THE BIG IDEAS BOOK

#1 INTERNATIONAL BEST SELLER

7 Powerful Marketing Strategies for the Modern World

THE BIG IDEAS BOOK

7 Powerful Marketing Strategies for the Modern World

SCOTT BYWATER
JOHN NORTH | ALAN CARNIOL | PETER BUTLER
MELANIE MACDONALD | KEITH BANFIELD | ARI GALPER

© Copyright 2024
By Scott Bywater, John North, Alan Carniol, Peter Butler,
Melanie MacDonald, Keith Banfield, Ari Galper

Edited by James North
All rights reserved.
Book Layout ©2024
Published by: Evolve Global Publishing
www.EvolveGlobalPublishing.com

No part of this book may be reproduced or transmitted in any form or by any means, electronic or mechanical, including photocopying, recording or by any information storage and retrieval system, without written permission from the authors, except for the inclusion of brief quotations in a review.

Limit of Liability Disclaimer: The information contained in this book is for information purposes only, and may not apply to your situation. The author, publisher, distributor, and provider provide no warranty about the content or accuracy of the content enclosed. The information provided is subjective. Keep this in mind when reviewing this guide. Neither the Publisher nor the Author shall be liable for any loss of profit or any other commercial damages resulting from the use of this guide. All links are for information purposes only and are not warranted for content, accuracy, or any other implied or explicit purpose.

Earnings Disclaimer: All income examples in this book are examples. They are not intended to represent or guarantee that everyone will achieve the same results. You understand that each individual's success will be determined by his or her desire, dedication, background, effort, and motivation to work. There is no guarantee you will duplicate any of the results stated here. You recognize any business endeavours have inherent risk or loss of capital.

The Big Ideas Book: 7 Powerful Marketing Strategies for the Modern World
1st Edition. 2024 V3

ASIN: B0CW19V188 (Amazon Kindle)
ISBN: 978-1-923223-01-1 (eBook)
ISBN: 978-1-923223-02-8 (Amazon Paperback)
ISBN: 978-1-923223-04-2 (Amazon Hardcover)
ISBN: 978-1-923223-03-5 (Ingram Spark) PAPERBACK
ISBN: 978-1-923223-05-9 (Ingram Spark) HARDCOVER
ISBN: 978-1-923223-01-1 (Smashwords/Barnes & Noble, Apple, Google Books)

Fonts:
HEADER: Avenir Black 24pt
CONTENT: Palatino 11pt

CONTACT THE AUTHOR
Business Name: Elite Marketers
Contact: www.elitemarketers.com.au
Email: helpme@elitemarketers.com.au

TRADEMARKS
All product names, logos, and brands are the property of their respective owners. All company, product, and service names used in this book are for identification purposes only. Using these names, logos, and brands does not imply endorsement. All other trademarks cited herein are the property of their respective owners.

Join Elite Marketers—an exclusive global community where top-tier marketing professionals converge to share insights, collaborate on innovative projects, and shape the future of the industry. Gain unparalleled access to expert insights, exclusive resources, and unmatched networking opportunities. Participate in members-only webinars and events to stay ahead of trends and elevate your marketing skills. Membership is typically by invitation or referral, but ambitious marketers can apply to join this visionary community. Take the next step in your marketing journey and join us to reach the highest level of excellence.

TABLE OF CONTENTS

About the Authors 1
Introduction 3
Scott Bywater: *Book Your Calendar Solid With Speed Emails Written by A.I* 7
John North: *Think Like Your Own Media Company* 27
Alan Carniol: *Winning More Dream Clients* 45
Peter Butler: *Building the Machine* 59
Melanie MacDonald: *Scaling Up Without Melting Down - Using Automation the Smart Way* 75
Keith Banfield: *Converting Leads Into Clients* 89
Ari Galper: *How To Unlock Your Sales Game!* 103
Conclusion 115
Glossary of Terms 119
Index 123
THE BIG IDEAS DAY 125
Where To From Here? 127

ABOUT THE AUTHORS

Scott Bywater
Founder of Copywriting That Sells & Elite Marketers

John North
CEO of Evolve Systems Group
10 Time #1 Best Selling Author (Amazon, USA Today and Wall Street Journal)

Alan Carniol
Coach and Author

Peter Butler
Digital Marketer | Serial Business Systemiser

Melanie MacDonald
Investor and Business Advisor

Keith Banfield
Coach, Author and Professional Speaker

Ari Galper
The World's Number One Authority on Trust-Based Selling

INTRODUCTION

BY SCOTT BYWATER

"Everything that can be invented has been invented."

These are the words that rolled from the mouth of Charles Holland Duell, the Commissioner of the United States Patent Office from 1898 to 1901. He even said the patent office would shrink in size, and eventually close.

Obviously, he was wrong. Dead wrong.

Over the past couple of decades, we've seen big ideas revolutionise the world: from Apple's iPhone to Uber's ride-sharing service to ChatGPT.

Yet what about those big, everyday ideas that can give your business an edge?

As a struggling entrepreneur, I remember being handed an idea from an internet marketing coach in my early days:

- Create a squeeze page
- Build an email list
- Send weekly emails

I received another idea from Matt Furey about sending daily emails - and exactly how to do it.

Those two ideas were the difference that made the difference during the early part of my career, helping me build a tribe and establish my authority.

I had another idea in 2019, of starting a group that's now called Elite Marketers.

It was based on reading Jayson Gaignard's book Mastermind Dinners and the 'aha' moment I received while on an 'artists date' with myself (an idea I got from Julia Cameron in her book The Artist's Way) that I didn't just sell to people; I sold through people. i.e., some of my best leads were as a result of the industry networks I had built.

This combination of ideas has been worth millions of dollars. In fact, they're the reason you're reading this book today.

It's also why we've called this book 'The Big Ideas Book.'

Of course, you'll need to work hard to make your ideas a reality. But make no mistake: One idea inside these pages can be the catalyst for generating more high-quality leads, closing tens of thousands of dollars in additional sales, and even building the foundational systems & infrastructure so you can 10x your business.

In the first chapter, I'll discuss how to book your calendar solid with speed emails written by AI and, more importantly, the formula for actually turning those emails into booked appointments with highly qualified prospects.

In the second chapter, John North shares how to think like and run a media company. In the 21st century, there's no better way to build trust. You'll also discover how to use social media to amplify your content rather than relying on it as your core focus.

In the third chapter, Alan Carniol reveals how to leverage Pareto's 80/20 principle to attract more of your best customers and eliminate 'bad fit' clients before they even walk through your door. How much time and frustration would that save you, and what would it do for your bottom line?

In the fourth chapter, Peter Butler explains how he manages to work primarily 'on' the business rather than 'in' it. Remember, you can only scale to the quality of your systems, and Peter lives and breathes this on a daily basis.

In the fifth chapter, Melanie MacDonald reveals how to scale operations without sacrificing your sanity. Mel is on the leading edge of AI and the latest technology, so if you're looking for enhanced efficiency pay close attention to everything she has to say.

In the sixth chapter, Keith Banfield explores the psychology behind effective selling. He debunks the myth of the "born salesperson" and introduces the M.A.N. Roadmap, which streamlines the focus on prospects who are most likely to convert.

Finally, in the seventh chapter, Ari Galper (the world's leading authority on trust-based selling) dismantles traditional sales paradigms with his Unlock the Game ® strategy, challenging aggressive sales tactics that prioritise closing deals over building genuine relationships.

This book is structured in a very specific way.

It starts with outside-the-box strategies for generating high-quality leads.

Then, it moves on to how to build capacity so you can actually scale to the next level.

And finally, it ends with guiding you on how to turn those leads into sales.

It's like a 3 legged stool. If you skip one (lead generation, systems, or sales) your business will be unbalanced. But combine them together, and they're like rocket fuel.

Within the pages ahead, you'll get a taste of the collective wisdom of the Elite Marketers tribe. Make no mistake, every author in this book can add value to your business, and help take it to the next level.

As you turn each page, remember that one idea, one strategy, or one new perspective can ignite a chain reaction of success. I look forward to hearing how a 'big idea' inside this book has propelled your business (and your life) to a level beyond what you thought possible.

About Elite Marketers

In recent decades, marketing has become more overwhelming and splintered than ever. It could be compared to a building site, where a variety of trades need to collaborate to build a home (or a skyscraper).

Today, there are many specialised skills needed ranging from PPC (Facebook ads, Google ads, Linkedin ads, etc), social media management (TikTok, Instagram, Facebook, Linkedin, Twitter, YouTube, etc), email marketing, automation, podcasting, mobile marketing (SMS, app-based marketing), conversion rate optimisation, content marketing (blogging, webinars, infographics, e-books), influencer marketing, affiliate marketing, video production, data analytics, brand management, reputation marketing, event marketing (virtual and in-person events), public relations, and community management amongst others.

Today, marketing requires a team, and joining Elite Marketers gives seasoned marketing professionals the opportunity to exchange ideas, gain a wider perspective, and connect with like-minded experts.

Likewise, business owners who engage the Elite Marketers community have the opportunity to receive a tailored service, working with leaders in their individual areas of expertise—leveraging a similar approach as a builder uses to construct a skyscraper.

To find out more about Elite Marketers visit www.elitemarketers.com.au or scan the QR Code below:

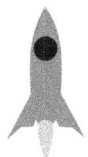

BOOK YOUR CALENDAR SOLID WITH SPEED EMAILS WRITTEN BY A.I

Scott Bywater
Founder of Copywriting That Sells & Elite Marketers

ABOUT THE AUTHOR: SCOTT BYWATER

Scott Bywater is among Australia's leading direct-response copywriters and the founder of Elite Marketers, one of the nation's top private marketing groups.

He created the 'Simple Email ROI System,' an online course that draws from his 21 years of experience in writing direct response copy for well-known figures and companies including Kerwin Rae, Knowledge Source (Jon Giaan), Jay Conrad Levinson (of 'Guerilla Marketing' fame), Mercola.com, and The Learning Annex.

His expertise also makes him a sought-after speaker. He has presented at events including James Schramko's SuperFast Business and Masterminds organised by Dale Beaumont, Ben Simkin, Andrew Sparks, and Francesca Moi. Scott's goal is to assist business owners in making the most of their email lists in a way that feels natural and straightforward, avoiding aggressive sales tactics.

Scott's work stands out because of his strategic approach to marketing. He focuses on leveraging email lists to build strong connections with audiences via the 'third-way' technique, emphasising the importance of genuine engagement over the 'hard sell.' His methods show that understanding and serving your audience's needs can lead to more high-quality leads and clients.

By prioritising clear and direct communication, Scott helps his clients and students achieve success without resorting to pushy sales tactics. His contributions to the marketing field, particularly in leveraging email lists, have proven effective for businesses looking to book their calendar solid.

Scott is on the leading edge, quickly adapting to the fast-changing digital environment. For instance, his use of AI tools in the 'Simple Email ROI System' is focused on helping his clients write in their own voice, based on their hard-won knowledge, without sounding like a robot.

According to Scott: "This is the key to setting yourself apart in a world where AI content is becoming the norm."

He believes true mastery lies in empathy, and focusing on the human element.

"Before writing anything, AI or otherwise, the most important thing we can do is to understand the conversation going on in our prospect's mind at a level where we can genuinely connect with the reader," he says.

Facebook, Google, Linkedin, YouTube, SEO, Snapchat, Instagram, TikTok…

You've been led to believe social media is where the action is at, yet the email marketing 'ugly duckling' is still the most effective way to generate leads and clients.

In fact, according to Litmus.com, the return on investment is:

$36 for every $1 invested

This far exceeds other marketing mediums. For instance, the Gignux Market Data Report 2024 found social media received a 250% return(1), and Google pay-per-click ads generate a 200% ROI, according to a recent report by Hubspot(2).

Now paid ads may be the perfect model for scaling.

For instance, one of my past clients has built a multi-million dollar business by sending prospects from paid ads to webinars or live events.

But guess how most marketers leverage those paid ads?
By getting them to join their email list and then nurturing that list to turn them into clients… or upselling them to the next stage of the sales cycle.

In this chapter, you'll discover how ChatGPT can help you write high-conversion emails fast, without sounding like a robot.

However, before I get to that, I need to squash a few myths that will prevent you from leveraging emails in the first place.

Let's start by breaking down the 6 reasons why email marketing is still one of the most effective marketing mediums today:

1. **You own 100% of the reader's attention:** You're not competing with hundreds of other brands because you're reaching out to customers 1 on 1.
2. **You're in control:** A simple algorithm shift cannot make your brand disappear overnight.
3. **It's more cost-effective:** While advertising on big tech platforms costs money (and those prices are rising monthly), email is virtually free.
4. **Guaranteed delivery:** If you're leveraging social posts, you never know when your followers will see them - whereas email virtually guarantees delivery to their inbox.
5. **It's personalised:** So the emails are more relevant and interesting to your recipients, which increases the odds they'll 'click' and take action.
6. **It's easy to measure:** You can track the number of people who open and click your emails, providing valuable insights into what's working and what isn't.

Yet most people don't leverage their email list because they think it's too small.

Let me explain why it's not:

Recently I talked to a colleague who does joint ventures with dozens of list owners, and he shared that he has achieved far greater results from a list of less than 50 people than he did from a list of 25,000+.

Likewise, I once completed a launch where I received 80% of the sales from a list of 200 paid subscribers… and only 20% of the sales from the other 6800 names on the list.

That's right:
- 32 sales out of 200 names - about 16%
- 8 sales out of 6800 names - 0.117%

That's a 136x Greater Response From the Most Loyal People on My List

Make no mistake, the success of email marketing isn't about the size of your list; it's about the depth of the relationship.

So, if you have a client list with whom you've built relationships over a period of years, you may be looking a gift horse in the mouth.

But I send out emails Scott, and all I get is crickets?

Whereas on socials, you get likes and comments on most posts, right?

It feels good. And you get a dopamine hit to your brain.

But there's a big difference between likes and sales.

For instance, I'll often send out emails and get zero comments.

Yet recently I ran a webinar with a joint venture partner.

It was about 4-5 emails encouraging people to join us.

27 registered for the event.

13 turned up.

7 of the 13 bought.

The event generated about $21,000, and I made over $8,000 in commissions.

Now my email list is about 1800 people, so that equates to…

$11.66 in Revenue for Every Name on the List

Now if you're like most people, you're probably worried about losing credibility by making offers. Or perhaps you fret about prospects or customers unsubscribing.

But you can sell via email without being pushy and while consistently delivering value.

While many self-proclaimed gurus say 'hitting your list' with aggressive offers on a regular basis is a good thing, this is what I refer to as the "scorched earth" approach.

It leads to soaring unsubscribe rates and list churn, literally killing the "golden goose" as your reputation and brand are tarnished.

The other email marketing camp is "The Romantics"…

Now "The Romantics" believe that to include any offer at all in an email communication should be avoided…

So they write the equivalent of "love letters" that contain no offers or "call to action" whatsoever.

They believe that sending out this endless content is a good thing and if they just keep writing, sales will magically appear. Nothing could be further from the truth…

This is an Unpredictable, Inconsistent and Painfully Slow Marketing Strategy

What I'd like to share with you is a completely different approach. I call it The Third Way…

The 3rd Way

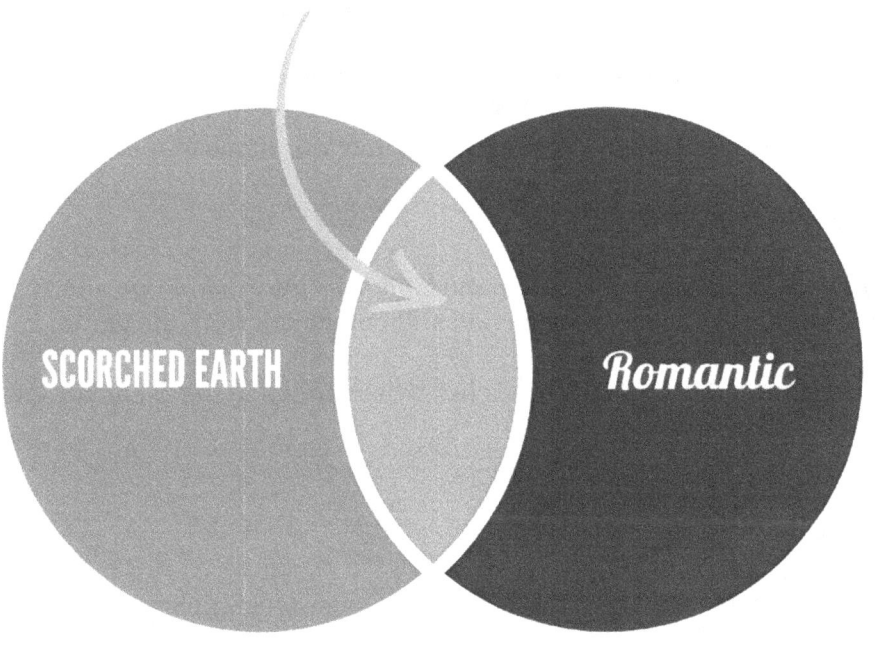

It's a fast and authentic method of building trust with high-value clients, where the most important component is writing offers that generate results - without burning your list to the ground.

Truth is, you have to make offers.

Otherwise, you won't sell anything. However, if you want to work with high-value clients and produce marketing your mother would be proud of, you need to do it appropriately.

The First Component of "The Third Way" is "Open Loop Offers"

These offers allow you to lead with high-value content at the beginning before segueing into a soft pitch at the end of your email. This means your readers will always appreciate seeing your name in their inbox.

Let's look at an example:

Cameron Strachan from Automatic Golf sells information products that help golfers get deeper satisfaction and enjoyment from the game.

We split-tested two emails to his list, by sending half the list email 1, and the other half email 2.

Here's the first email:

SUBJECT: The '4% Thinking Secret' for Consistent Ball Striking

Hi NAME,

What if adding raw power to your swing and mind-blowing consistency to your overall game…

Was as simple as flicking on a 'thinking switch?'
Let me explain…

You've probably heard of the Pareto Principle…

And the fact that for many events, about 80% of the effects come from 20% of the causes.

It was discovered by Vilfred Pareto who found that 20% of Italians owned 80% of the wealth.

But the principle repeats itself in all things - nature, business and yes...

EVEN GOLF.

And it's fractal - meaning just 4% of your activities generate 64% of your results.

Below is one of the most important graphs that helps explain the Pareto Principle and how you can get better results with the least amount of stress and effort.

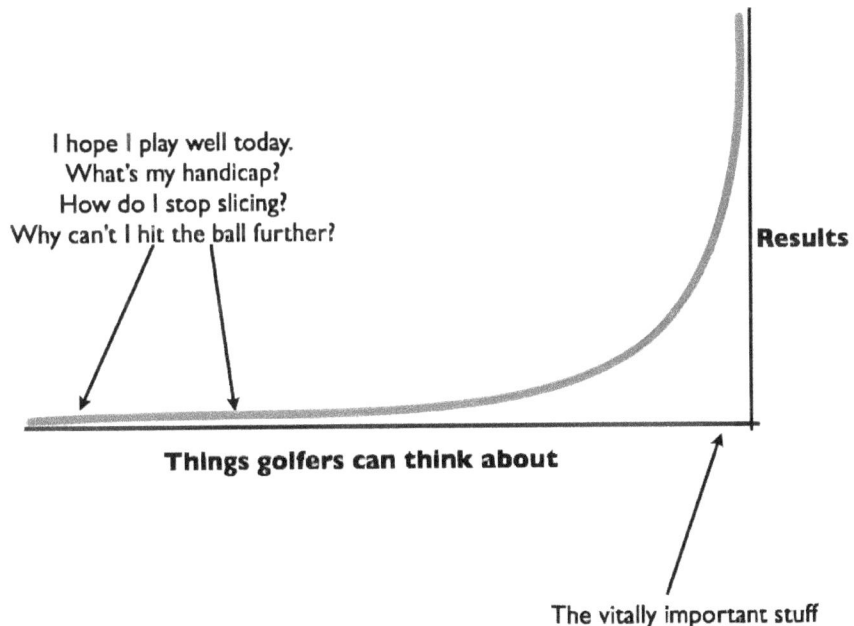

Bottom line: If you focus on the really important stuff you'll get a breakthrough.

Yet this is easier said than done, because most golfers struggle to stop thinking about all the rubbish. Yes, they're constantly thinking about:
- *Their grip*
- *Stance*
- *Swing plane*
- *Forearm plane*
- *Body pivot*
- *Wrist cock*
- *Weight shift*
- *Backswing length*

Yet for the most part, thinking about these things will slow you down.

They make golf hard, not easier.

That's why I created the **Automatic Golf Bible**

Make no mistake - if you can leave thoughts about your technique alone, you'll have a breakthrough.

You'll also light your learning system on fire and it will reward you with better golf.

The key is to simplify.

To think less and not more.

Like to know how, so you can hit every tee shot further and unleash true consistency?

Then check out the **Automatic Golf Bible** now.

You'll be glad you did :)

Cameron Strachan

Now the second email is exactly the same, except there's a "twist" at the end. Here's the close we used…

Yet for the most part, thinking about these things will slow you down.

They'll make your golf harder, not easier.

In fact. if you can do just ONE THING with your thinking, you'll have a breakthrough.

You'll also light your learning system on fire - and this will reward you with better golf.

The question is… what is this ONE THING the best golfers in the world know about, that almost everyone else is oblivious to?

I pondered this question for years.

And I've finally found the solution, which I'm opening the lid on in The Automatic Golf Bible.

It's so simple, you'll kick yourself when you hear it.

And yet it will literally make you…

Hit your Tee Shots further and straighter into the fairway (and into play)

Nail down your accuracy, so you automatically stop slicing, hooking, duffing or shanking.

Ensure your clubhead is naturally in the ideal position through impact.

And all this will give you an injection of confidence so strong, you'll be able to play the best golf of your life!

Like to know the "ONE THING" thinking secret elite golfers swear by?

*Then grab **The Automatic Golf Bible** now.*

You'll be glad you did :)

Cameron Strachan

Guess which email performed the best?

That's right, it was email #2.

In fact, email 1 made 5 sales @ $97, generating $485 in revenue...

Whereas email 2 - with the open loop offer - made 9 sales @ $97, generating $873 in revenue.

That's an 80% Better Conversion Rate, All Thanks to the Open Loop Offer

Imagine sending three emails like this a week.

As you can see, these deceptively simple 'open loop offers' are a fun and irresistible way to turn every piece of email communication into a highly effective sales machine.

You can't not know, right? You have to click to find out the answer!

It's like turning off the TV two minutes before the end of a Game of Thrones episode. Not going to happen, is it?

You always want to resolve the story bouncing around in your brain.

And it's not just Game of Thrones...

What does every single TV show end on? A cliffhanger to the next episode.

They never resolve the story.

Same with every single morning show, just before the ad break.

It's the one technique used across every single genre.

And you don't have to stop with the offer - you can also leverage a 'second open loop' to get your readers excited about the next email. Here's an example:

P.S. In my next email, I'm going to explain how to take a simple product – like a piece of metal – and sell over 300 million units. Believe me, you won't want to miss the important lesson it contains. Stay tuned :)

In case you're wondering if 'open loop offers' will work in your industry, here are some examples of different open loop offers in wildly different businesses that can be used towards the end of the email…

Accounting SAAS Platform

Did you know there's a simple way to check how much more profitable you were this year than last year?

And it takes just 10 seconds.

In fact, you can press just one button within X, Y, Z software.

Would you like to know what that button is?

Then click here

YouTube Ads Online Course

There's a simple YouTube script I'm using right now, with almost all of my students, which is generating double the average results.

And it applies to virtually every industry.

Yet it's so simple. In fact, it's just 17 words.

Would you like to know what those words are?

You'll find them in the first module of my FREE Mastering Youtube course, which you can grab here.

Property Investing Event

Right now, there are seven under-the-radar suburbs in Sydney where all the metrics suggest you can buy a house at 17-27% under market value.

Most real estate agents don't know about them. Same with mortgage brokers.

In fact, 99 out of 100 people are completely oblivious.

I've kept them close to my chest until now, however, I'll be sharing what they are - and the pockets within those suburbs that offer the highest rental returns - when you join me at the Property Investors Location Summit this Saturday.

Bottom line: If you have a list of names… and a product or service of any kind… 'Open Loop Offers' will work for you, no matter what industry you're in.

Ok, so now we've worked out that email works, and we know how to structure them without being pushy - you're probably wondering… what on earth am I going to write about?

Maybe you're struggling here, because you think your industry is too boring.

Now let me introduce you to a process that will blow your mind.

AI streamlines all of this, just think of it as your assistant content writer.

Simply go to Chat GPT right now and type this prompt in:

Prompt 1: Act as a world class market research expert. Please list the top 5 fears people have about hiring a [YOUR PROFESSION]

For instance: Act as a world class market research expert. Please list the top 5 fears people have about hiring a real estate agent to sell their property.

Here's the response from ChatGPT:

1. **High Commission Fees:** One of the primary concerns is the cost of hiring a real estate agent, specifically the commission fees, which typically range from 5% to 6% of the sale price in many markets. Sellers fear that these fees might significantly reduce their profit from the sale.

2. **Lack of Control:** Sellers often worry about losing control over the selling process when they hire an agent. This includes concerns about the marketing strategy, pricing decisions, and the negotiation process with potential buyers.

3. **Inadequate Communication:** There's a fear that once an agent is hired, they might not communicate regularly or effectively, leaving the seller out of the loop on important developments, showings, feedback from potential buyers, or changes in the market that could affect the sale.

4. **Questionable Loyalty and Effort:** Sellers are sometimes concerned that an agent might not have their best interests at heart or may not put in the necessary effort to get the best price for the property. This fear is compounded if the agent is managing multiple listings and may prioritize some over others.

5. **Mismatched Expectations:** There's a fear that the real estate agent may not fully understand or align with the seller's goals, whether it's the timeline for selling, the desired sale price, or specific conditions of the sale. This can lead to frustration and disappointment if the property sells for less than expected or takes longer to sell than anticipated.

After uncovering these fears, I can then ask for a 1-month content plan with the following prompt:

Prompt 2: Based on these 5 fears, act as a world-class email marketing expert and create a one-month content plan that includes 3 emails a week.

Here's the response I received back:

Week 1: Understanding Real Estate Commissions

Email 1: Introduction to Real Estate Commissions: What You Need to Know

Email 2: How Real Estate Commissions Work and Where Your Money Goes

Email 3: Tips for Negotiating Commissions with Your Real Estate Agent

Week 2: Maintaining Control Throughout the Selling Process

Email 1: How to Stay in Control During the Selling Process

Email 2: Your Role vs. Your Agent's Role: A Partnership in Selling Your Home

Email 3: Case Study: Successful Seller Experiences and How They Maintained Control

Week 3: Ensuring Effective Communication

Email 1: The Importance of Communication in Real Estate Transactions

Email 2: Setting Expectations: How Often Should You Hear from Your Real Estate Agent?

Email 3: Tools and Techniques for Effective Seller-Agent Communication

Week 4: Loyalty and Effort: Choosing the Right Agent

Email 1: How to Assess a Real Estate Agent's Loyalty and Commitment

Email 2: The Signs of a Hard-Working Real Estate Agent

Email 3: Real Stories: How the Right Agent Made All the Difference

Ok, so we now have a content calendar, but how do you write emails that are unique to you... and which don't sound like a robot?

That's where our next piece of magic is: the AI transcription assistant otter.ai, which you can download onto your phone and computer.

It will transcribe what you say, so you can enter it into ChatGPT and have it write an email based on your knowledge and experience.

After completing the transcript in Otter, here's the prompt you want to enter into ChatGPT:

Prompt 3: I want to create an email about the signs of a hard-working real estate agent. I want to read it off as a transcript and then feed the transcript back into ChatGPT. Act as if you are a world-class copywriter, like Gary Bencivenga. Provide 3 bullet points I should talk about to create the transcript.

The response I received back from ChatGPT was:

1. **Proactive Communication:** A hard-working real estate agent doesn't just respond to inquiries or concerns; they anticipate them. They keep you informed with regular updates, sharing insights about the market, feedback from showings, and changes in the competitive landscape. This proactive approach ensures you're always in the loop and confident in your agent's commitment to selling your property.

2. **Customised Marketing Strategies:** Rather than relying on a one-size-fits-all approach, a diligent agent crafts a tailored marketing plan for your property. They understand the unique selling points of your home and leverage a mix of traditional and digital marketing tools to reach the right audience. This includes professional staging, high-quality photography, social media promotion, and networking with potential buyers and other agents.

3. **Persistence and Adaptability:** The real estate market is dynamic, and challenges are inevitable. A hard-working agent demonstrates resilience by adapting strategies as needed and tirelessly working to overcome obstacles. Whether it's adjusting the listing price, revisiting the marketing approach, or negotiating with potential buyers, their persistent effort is aimed at achieving the best possible outcome for you.

Now all a real estate agent would need to do would be to talk about these points for 1-3 minutes into Otter. And then drop it into the final prompt:

Prompt 4: Great. Act as a world-class copywriter and write an email of approximately 300-500 words about why email is still relevant. Here is the transcript to base the email off: [INSERT THE TRANSCRIPT HERE].

Ok, during this chapter, we have covered:
- Why you should take email marketing seriously (it gets a 36 to 1 ROI on investment)
- Why your email list is not too small
- How to sell via email without being pushy via the third way
- Examples of open loop offers
- How to get ChatGPT to help you create a monthly content plan.
- How to write emails that sound like you, not like a robot.

I'd love to dive deeper and show you a live example where I actually create the transcript with otter, and then feed it into ChatGPT - so you can see the emails written in real time.

I'd also like to walk you through my PDF strategy, so you can discover exactly how to create an avalanche of free reports and landing pages, and segment your list to book your calendar solid:

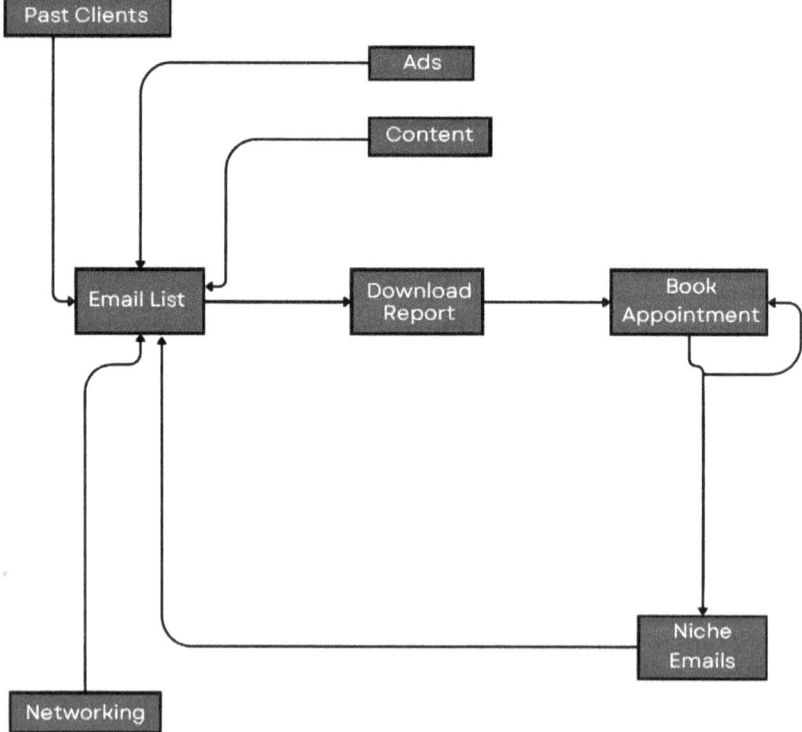

However, I'm running out of space here, so here's a free bonus.

Recently, I completed a presentation for Dale Beaumont's high-level mastermind where I broke this entire strategy down, including the exact prompt stack I used, and a swipe file for the landing page and appointment booking page.

I also revealed exactly how to create a lead magnet for your business. If you'd like to get free access, simply visit: https://www.simpleemailroi.com/ai-training2 or scan:

SCOTT BYWATER
Founder of Copywriting That Sells & Elite Marketers

https://EvolveGlobalPublishing.com/s/scott-bywater

Citations:
https://gitnux.org/social-media-marketing-roi-statistics/#:~:text=The%20average%20ROI%20for%20social,media%20conversion%20rate%20was%209.3%25
https://blog.hubspot.com/marketing/ppc-statistics#:~:text=Google%20pay%2Dper%2Dclick%20ads,global%202.purchases%20take%20place%20online

THINK LIKE YOUR OWN MEDIA COMPANY

John North
CEO of Evolve Systems Group
10 Time #1 Best Selling Author (Amazon, USA Today and Wall Street Journal)

ABOUT THE AUTHOR: JOHN NORTH

Transforming Entrepreneurs through Cutting-Edge Publishing and Software Solutions...

People regard John North as a versatile and experienced entrepreneur with a solid background in Accounting, Banking, Business Management, Finance, Personal Development, IT, Software, and Strategic Marketing.

John has written ten #1 Best-Selling Books about book publishing, business strategy and internet marketing, and a book about Squash.

John is the CEO of Evolve Systems Group. He is a serial entrepreneur who has created many products and services that empower business owners and entrepreneurs. Some of these ventures include: Evolve Global Publishing, Evolvepreneur®.app,, Evolve Your Business, and Evolve Mobile.

John is passionate about helping business owners become smarter and more strategic about their marketing efforts. His peers widely regard him as very innovative and highly creative in his approach because he constantly pushes the envelope of what's possible in this modern era.

Evolve Global Publishing is a premium service John created to enable him to help thousands rather than hundreds of entrepreneurs. He believes anyone can follow a system to success, but the missing keys are implementation and accountability. The Evolve Global Publishing platform and its methodologies allow an entrepreneur and potential author to create and publish their own book in a little as 90 days without writing a single word!

His latest venture, Evolvepreneur®.app, is an all-in-one platform designed to allow entrepreneurs to take control of their future and to be less reliant on using social media for managing their business online.

John lives in Sydney, Australia with his wife and son and plays competitive squash 5 days a week.

John is an expert in quick start concepts for online entrepreneurs. His accomplishments include:

- Over 30 years in business and online marketing
- Over 25 million worth of sales for himself and clients in 35 years
- Written 10 #1 Best Selling business books
- Published or been involved in over 1,500 books
- Won Australia Day Award for my shire back in 1984
- Worked as an ambulance officer
- Was part of the state emergency service
- Was policeman for his town for 2 days
- Took over failing accounting software distribution company and turned them into #2 distributor in the world in 3 years
- "Built a powerful game-changing 'SaaS' business growth and marketing platform from the ground up

Like me, as an entrepreneur, you're always searching for new opportunities, which is why the internet became so popular so fast.

From my perspective, the dominance of "big tech" has transformed the game, with few recognizing the potential hazards.

It's clear that over the past decade or so, these once-small companies that started in garages and bedrooms have strategically evolved. Their goal was to collect as much personal data as possible into large systems, which they can now further enhance with A.I.

They want you to create continuous content and ensure user engagement on their platform. They have the power to punish you, including taking away your accounts and followers, all in the name of upholding their "community standards."

Your success depends on the continual generation of content for these platforms, but this task has increasingly become less effective.

Social Media Marketing can be a soul-destroying game, ensnaring individuals and businesses in a perpetual cycle of content creation for the sake of staying current.

Given the rise of Artificial Intelligence (AI) and automation, achieving long-term victory in the game seems unlikely.

Picture this happening to you…

I woke up one morning to read an email about the news that LinkedIn has decided to terminate my account, stating that this resolution is final, and there is no point in attempting to regain access.

When I had asked an employee to check my profile and posts, I discovered that the platform mysteriously disappeared all of my content and communication.

That's 15 years of posts, gone forever!

Losing over 30,000 LinkedIn connections was a real possibility for me, and I accepted I might never get them back!

It took weeks and several emails with their support department, but I finally recovered my account.

There seems to have been a confusion between me and the BOTS!

One advantage of LinkedIn over other social media platforms is its personal support and the only reason I got back my account.

When I decided to cancel my Premium Membership, I had to endure the same process all over again a month later because they resumed their pursuit once I stopped paying. Eventually, I gave in and agreed to pay again, but I haven't heard a word from them since.

In my mind, this is no way to run a business!

It got me thinking about what I would do if LinkedIn or Facebook terminated me again. This wasn't the first time I'd had this conversation.

This made me realise it might be a good idea to move away from social media platforms, which are always changing, and to explore alternative strategies for growth and impact.

For a long time, experts have promoted social media platforms as the ideal platforms for digital marketing and brand development.

Despite that, the landscape is transforming for several reasons.

Privacy concerns erode trust in these platforms, changing consumer behaviours, hate speech, and "fake news".

If you find yourself in one of the following scenarios (like me), then it's time to reassess your current strategy:

- You are facing difficulties in generating revenue from an online business or social media following.

- Despite having a substantial social media following, you struggle to convert them into paying customers.
- You are a specialist and want to expand your current high-touch business into an online one to generate more revenues
- Many websites, plugins, and access points spread out your online business, creating a fragmented and complicated customer journey.
- You are in the medical or other heavily regulated industries and struggle to expand your skills to a broader audience.

You are not alone.

The traditional route endorsed by social media and internet marketing experts has turned out to be an illusion, leaving people trapped in a cycle of over-dependence and disappointment.

Consider the idea that social media platforms and internet marketers could have steered you in the wrong direction. You are now up against automated intelligence that can generate large volumes of content and video in minutes when it would take days or weeks in the past.

A.I. has had a profound impact on the landscape of digital marketing and content creation.

The increasing role of AI in automating tasks and generating large-scale content presents a fresh set of opportunities and challenges.

This challenge for visibility and engagement raises a crucial question.

Is investing in this relentless content creation race the best way to leverage knowledge and grow a business?

Sure, you can play this A.I. game too, but is it the optimal strategy for leveraging your knowledge and expanding your business? What if you seriously entertained the idea of "flipping the game"? The distinction between getting lost in the online noise and finding success lies in changing your perspective to become an autonomous media entity.

Have you ever thought about acting as your own media company and having complete ownership of your content?

To make this idea work, you'll have to change your strategy and thinking completely. Imagine if you directed your efforts towards growing or launching your own online business independently, without relying on social media, and instead built your own Brand Media Company/Platform. To achieve online business growth and independence from social media, it's important not to depend solely on it.

Instead, build your own "platform".

Consider this…

Social media plays a secondary role in customer service for the world's most prosperous companies. Consider the electric car manufacturer, Tesla, for instance, who lists no social media links on their website.

You can't take followers to the bank and get cash for them.

Social media platforms work against you, not for you, because they want their visitors to stay on their platform and not go to your site.

If you are not paying, you are the product!

Email and SMS remain the most profitable and cost-effective marketing methods for marketers if appropriately leveraged. In fact, social media platforms rely on emails to drive engagement.

Check out any conventional news or information outlet.

These outlets use social media to drive traffic to their website, strategically posting limited content that compels viewers to visit for further details.

Later on, their goal is to persuade you to subscribe or consume more content in order to keep you engaged.

There's no better way to make a lasting impact on the world than by driving traffic to your website and converting it into subscribers or viewers.

Actionable Strategy: Create your own email list that is under your control.

As lifestyles evolve and new platforms rise, the content consumption landscape undergoes a transformation.

In a world where free time is scarce, traditional and digital platforms face difficulties in capturing and keeping people's attention.

Platforms like TikTok have revolutionised content consumption by catering to the modern audience's shrinking attention spans with their short and engaging formats.

Because of the shift, people have changed how they consume content and spend their time online. They now want a focused, personalised experience.

Facebook is now experiencing the impact of these more agile rivals, despite being the undisputed leader in social media.

The emergence of these platforms is causing a shift in attention and engagement away from traditional news channels and long-standing social media networks.

This evolution in consumer behaviour underscores the necessity for businesses and content creators to adapt and rethink their strategies.

The focus is no longer solely on being present on the internet.

The best marketers don't rely solely on social media.

You have the power to control your words and audience, free from algorithm bans. Let's get back to the original question.

How do you "flip the game?"

Building Your Independent Digital Empire

Take these steps to learn how to think like and run your very own media company.

Develop a **robust online image** that resonates with your audience, focusing on personal and business branding. It is crucial that you keep a cohesive story throughout all your communication channels.

Create engaging content by launching a podcast that connects with your audience.

Make social media a secondary outlet for distributing your content, directing visitors back to your website or portal.

Generating revenue: Look into avenues like advertising, sponsorships, and memberships. Provide valuable incentives to persuade your audience to invest in your brand.

Make list building a priority by collecting as many email addresses and mobile numbers as you can.

Encourage the development of a community centred on your brand. Connect with your audience using newsletters, exclusive offers, and interactive content.

Take advantage of networks like LinkedIn to attract professional traffic and expand your subscriber base for content like podcasts, blogs, or newsletters.

I have some specific ideas that you should consider.

- Invite guests or host your own podcast/show.
- Create books that apply to your niche and can encourage participation in conversations with your primary audience.
- Make the most of your audience by offering advertising and sponsorship opportunities.
- Create a list of subscribers for a podcast, blog, or newsletter.
- Build email campaigns around your platform to bring subscribers to your site
- Generate custom outcomes through membership offers or solution-based surveys.

- Foster a community that shares your passion and belief in your mission/idea.
- Use affiliates and referral partners to increase website traffic.
- By training a Knowledge ChatBOT with your intellectual property, you can create valuable coaching or advice that can be used as either a front-end or back-end tool. It's possible that this could be a model based on subscriptions.

Check out https://evolvepreneur.media to understand our direction.

We blend news with our own content.

You can find our podcast shows on our show pages and we encourage subscribers to sign up for added bonuses and exclusive access.

Building Your Online Identity

The starting point of your journey lies in your digital identity. It incorporates your personal brand, business principles, and the exceptional value you bring to the table.

Creating consistency in branding, message, aesthetics, and values across all platforms builds trust with your audience. By conducting a brand audit, you can implement an actionable strategy. Review your online presence to make sure your messages and visuals align well.

In order to unify all channels, recognise inconsistencies and establish a strategy.

Content is the fundamental element.

On the internet, content is like currency. What makes you special is your skill in producing content that is relevant, valuable, and captivating.

Expand your reach and cater to different audience preferences by diversifying your content types, like blogs, videos, podcasts, or infographics.

As an illustrative example, a financial advisor, typically dependent on word-of-mouth referrals, establishes a blog to clarify personal finance.

With time, this blog can establish itself as a reliable resource, attracting visitors to their website to explore services, enroll in webinars, and join a subscription-based financial planning program.

Unlocking the full potential of social media

You should build your digital empire on a foundation that doesn't rely on social media.

Take advantage of these platforms to share excerpts of your content, engage in discussions, and drive traffic to your website or platform so people can enjoy the complete range of your offerings.

Take a practical approach: Develop content teasers on social media to spark interest and redirect followers to your website for the full experience. Ensure that your bio or posts include straightforward calls-to-action and easily navigable links.

Increasing Your Audience and Generating Income

The backbone of a media company is its loyal community. Connect with your audience by interacting, offering exclusives, and creating community-focused content.

Encourage your audience to give feedback and cultivate a sense of belonging.

Conduct live Q&A Sessions, launch community challenges, and highlight user-generated content on your platform.

Engage your current audience and draw in new members by organizing activities centred on shared values and interests.

Beyond Advertisements: Exploring Different Sources of Revenue

While advertising can bring in money, it's important to diversify for long-term financial stability.

Expand your income potential by exploring memberships, affiliate marketing, digital products, and consulting services.

As an illustrative example, a yoga instructor expands their business by offering a subscription-based online yoga series, private coaching sessions, and branded merchandise.

This diversification improves the community's perception of the brand and increases revenue.

Harness the Power of Technology to Gain a Competitive Advantage

In order to leave a lasting impression in the digital age, creativity alone is not enough; technological expertise is also crucial.

Take advantage of tools and technologies to streamline operations, enhance content, and customise audience experiences.

There are a lot of tools out there that serve as indispensable allies in gaining digital sovereignty, like SEO optimization and CRM systems to optimize content visibility and community engagement. Use analytics tools to understand your audience's behaviour and preferences.

Tailor your content and offerings based on these insights to increase engagement and conversion rates.

Nurturing Long-Term Relationships

Building a digital empire is a marathon, not a sprint.

Nurturing connections with your audience, collaborators, and even competitors can offer valuable support throughout your journey.

By being transparent, authentic, and consistent in your interactions, you can cultivate loyalty and advocacy in your community.

As an example: To expand their reach and create a sense of community, a tech blogger partners with fellow content creators for guest posts and webinars. Through newsletters and social media, they consistently interact with their audience, establishing an open dialogue and cultivating relationships that go beyond simple transactions.

Monitoring the Expansion of Your Digital Empire

Just like you, your digital empire will continue to grow. Being open-minded and ready to adjust in response to emerging trends, technologies, and audience demands is of utmost importance in this evolution.

Stay educated, stay curious, and be open to change as a crucial part of your journey. Conduct quarterly reviews of your content strategy, revenue streams, and audience engagement metrics. Use these insights to adapt your tactics, explore new opportunities, and phase out what's no longer effective.

The Ultimate System for Business Success and Marketing Strategies

Developing your own platform is the best way to set up a sustainable business focused on growth.

Achieve independence from "Big Tech" to avoid bans or throttling.

Make use of them to generate traffic for your assets, like a website, recurring membership, online shop, or e-learning platform, and establish your audience.

Based on my extensive experience as a marketing consultant, I have developed a blueprint for online entrepreneurs to succeed in today's competitive marketplace.

The **overall customer experience** should be your primary focus. Aim for a high level of minimal friction signup and embrace automation as often as you can.

Begin with a **mobile-friendly website** that combines your podcasts, videos, courses, memberships, and blogs.

Expand your subscriber database and automatically notify them of new content via email. The marketing module should send emails or take actions based on prospects' behaviour to guide them through your courses and products.

Design pages to grow your subscriber database by offering free checklists, blueprints, and/or ebooks. **Your website should allow visitors to buy** and manage the delivery of your products in one place.

Upsell products when customers check out. Categorising your prospects enables you to create powerful follow-up emails.

It's advisable to incorporate **multiple payment gateways.** When you grow quickly, incorporating multiple payment gateways reduces the risk of funds being held back by one portal. Offering products in various currencies can help minimize buyer resistance.

It might be beneficial to establish a **recurring membership system** for regular user billing and convenient record management.

While you may have different front-end websites in mind, it is important that they all direct back to your eCommerce and backend member area for seamless management. You can promote various aspects of your business **without dividing your audience or resources.**

If you want your business to thrive, developing an **affiliate program** is key. Encourage referrers or affiliates to spread the word about your products and services for rewards.

By the end of the process, customers should complete their initial journey in the back-end membership area, accessing their invoices, downloads, and bonus content. **Customers shouldn't have to navigate multiple websites to find this information!**

It is essential to implement a **ticketing system** or similar service system to assist your customers.

Create a secure login-based community that offers **extra value to clients and prospects**, fostering strong engagement and recurring visits for your content.

To better engage users, introduce **gamification features** such as status badges and rewards systems to your community.

Consider developing courses that allow your members to learn at their own pace online. Your course platform should enable them to advance gradually by completing each lesson, rather than following a weekly schedule that might cause them to fall behind and lose motivation. **Encourage students to interact and engage.**

What if downloading a worksheet PDF wasn't necessary? Users never finish it anyway! It's important to have a system in place that allows users to leave their responses while they complete the lessons. You can view all their responses and track their progress in the course. **This approach ensures that nobody is left behind!**

As your students progress through the course, you can assign tasks to them. **Consider creating a coaching program that aligns with their task list.**

You need a **robust analytics reporting system** that provides detailed insights on the sources of your traffic and their interactions, empowering you to make informed decisions for your marketing campaigns.

A **single dashboard** will be essential for monitoring statistics, generating content, and overseeing business operations.

It's ideal to **establish a procedure system** (Knowledge Base) for consistent execution of processes by your staff and contractors. Simplify creating step-by-step instructions instead of repeatedly training employees on the same processes.

Suppose you were interested in establishing a mastermind group? To achieve the best results, it's recommended to group individuals together and **give centralised access to Q&A calls, group tasks, and results**.

Making use of a **project management system** can aid you and your team in handling both your projects and those of your clients.

Consider the idea of **having control over your QR Codes** and being able to change them as needed.

What is the required time to achieve all of this?

Possibly a year or more!

I've wasted countless hours and spent a fortune trying to find a platform that has most of the features I want.

From what I could tell, that system doesn't seem to exist.

Out of frustration, I created a platform that caters to the needs of entrepreneurs, coaches, authors, podcasters, publishers, and mastermind groups.

I named it Evolvepreneur®.app. I am on a mission to spark a revolution that assists entrepreneurs in building their own all-encompassing business systems, capable of challenging mainstream social media platforms.

We've identified the key signals that are crucial for a successful platform deployment.

We built our platform for "content" and/or "products/services", with a focus on generating recurring revenues and automating customer service.

Podcasts, blogs, courses, Subscribers, Memberships, and Courses are the focal points of our platform.

Our platform owners require multiple websites to highlight important aspects of their business.

If you enjoy content creation and product development and require a simple management solution, we are the perfect platform for you.

You can choose to start off with a simple site, begin a podcast, or dive in by building a complete business system.

Startups are individuals like solopreneurs, coaches, consultants, or authors who aim to establish a presence and generate income.

The primary aim is to market your services and release a book and/or podcast. In addition, you're considering creating a membership or mastermind offer.

Despite being in operation for a while, you're still stuck in a growth phase because of multiple platforms and a complex mix of websites and offers.

Your overall plan requires resetting and refreshing. Your aim is to expand and automate for time and cost savings. Establish a consistent income flow by offering memberships, coaching, or consulting programs.

Your company is complex, so it requires a comprehensive assessment and relaunch, despite having all the traits of a "growth level."

You're interested in including all your existing contacts in a free and paid community.

The mastermind behind your digital kingdom.

Evolvepreneur®.app differentiates itself in a saturated digital landscape as the go-to platform for creating a cohesive online presence.

Evolvepreneur®.app is the all-in-one solution, born out of frustrations and limitations in digital marketing and online business operations.

Empower your online business with unmatched efficiency using this SaaS platform.

The King of all things is Owned Content.

We created content-based modules to help in various areas, such as:

- **Podcasting,** which allows you to host a show by yourself or with guests, with subscribers being notified of new episodes and syndicated across social media and podcast platforms through RSS feeds.
- **Blogs,** where you can post content and distribute it to subscribers while syndicating it to social media platforms through RSS feeds.

- **Community Groups**: concentrating content and processes in a central place for specific prospects or subscribers.

Navigating the Journey Towards Digital Sovereignty.

Adopting a media company's mindset causes a strategic change and a dedication to long-term growth.

The key is to establish a direct connection with your audience based on trust, value, and mutual respect.

The success of this approach relies on patience, consistency, and adaptability to the changing digital world.

Don't forget that independence doesn't equate to being alone as you embark on this journey.

Work together with colleagues, strategically use established platforms, and remain committed to your mission and values.

The digital empire you create now will be the legacy you leave behind, a testament to vision, perseverance, and independence in a connected world.

JOHN NORTH
CEO of Evolve Systems Group
10 Time #1 Best Selling Author (Amazon, USA Today and Wall Street Journal)

https://EvolveGlobalPublishing.com/s/john-north

WINNING MORE DREAM CLIENTS

Alan Carniol
Coach and Author

ABOUT THE AUTHOR: ALAN CARNIOL

Alan helps individuals and businesses find the special sauce that defines their unique brand. His superpower is connecting his clients' distinctive attributes with their target audiences' goals.

Alan started his professional life working as a consultant in public finance. There, he helped governments structure bond deals, trained new hires, and developed financial products.

Following his MBA, Alan launched three companies, one of which achieved success. His online business forced him to study direct response marketing. His work in professional development, specifically around the job search, honed his skills in personal marketing, branding, and storytelling. To further this work, Alan studied the hero's journey (seen in films such as Star Wars, Toy Story, and Princess Bride) and trained in professional coaching.

Alan has advised over a thousand professionals on career transitions and personal marketing. He has also helped small businesses to redesign their sales and marketing approach, leading to results such as doubling sales in 6 months, generating consistent 30% year-over-year growth, and enabling a struggling business to generate more leads and clients than it could handle.

Alan has been featured in Forbes, US News and World Report, Inc, and Fast Company, among others. He holds a BA in Psychology from the University of Pennsylvania and an MBA from Yale School of Management.

Alan hopes to have free time again someday. For now, he enjoys his young family.

Picture your best customer:

They love what you do. Before they met your business, they had a problem. They tried to solve it, but nothing else worked. Then they met your business. It was magic. From the beginning, they understood what you do. And they wanted it – badly. They pay in full without delay, and they think the value you deliver far exceeds the price. Serving them is easy. Your core offer just fits them. In fact, you have transformed their world, and they are grateful. And you feel joyful in how your business serves them.

Picture your worst customer:

They don't seem to fully understand your business or your product – or appreciate the value it brings. You spend time explaining, customizing, and fixing, and holding their hand. It's a battle to get information from them. They whine and complain. They want discounts and are slow to pay. And they stress you out and make you feel miserable.

What if you could line up more of your best customers and eliminate bad ones before they walk in your door?

My goals in this chapter are two-fold:

1. To instill the value of a focused marketing approach – attuned to your best customers
2. To give you the tools to get in sync with your best clients

Why does this matter?

The Pareto Principle recognizes the recurring pattern of the 80/20 distribution – in business, this implies our best 20% of customers yield 80% of profits (20% of this group, the top 4%, is responsible for 64% of profits; the top ~1% generates 50% of profits.) Research studies don't exactly match but are close, ranging from the top 20% responsible for 73% of profits to as much as 120% of profits. Whatever the exact numbers, if we focus on this small group of customers, we can see outsized growth in profits and have a happier business life.

On the flip side, the bottom 20% of customers is the source of 80% of headaches. In most cases, you lose money by serving them. We would do better if they go away.

Many business owners are afraid to take a stand and focus their marketing on their best clients. Maybe it feels elitist. Maybe their ego is tied up in supporting a sexy client segment that doesn't support business goals. Maybe they don't want to miss opportunities by focusing their message.

In the days of yore, there was some logic to this. Businesses had more limited reach. Advertising was hard to focus – billboards, newspapers, TV ads. At best, you could narrow attention to a specialized trade magazine or a direct mail list.

Not anymore. We live in a world of globally available resources, accessible from anywhere via the internet, where remote work is normal, and where AI-powered tools have brought personal customization to an unprecedented level.

This environment means that competition for customers has never been higher. Big brands that try to appeal to everyone often lose out. For example, Budweiser, the American "King of Beers" sold nearly 30 million beer barrels in 2003. Its business almost halved by 2013, overtaken by more tailored Craft breweries. It was nearly halved again in 2023.

Alternatively, big firms that won over the past decade were those that connected us to our unique individual wants:
- Airbnb (specific location, specific home type)
- Google (search for specific answers)
- Etsy (search for specific craft products)
- Uber (specific location for driver/specific food).

These businesses are getting challenged by even more tightly focused businesses serving more specific groups. (e.g. rideshare services for kids or for dogs, search engines with greater privacy or better personalization of results). Facebook, the titan designed so people can connect virtually with friends, has seen its market domination reduced by niche apps. On top of it, today's leading businesses are using AI to hyper-tailor their marketing.

That means, if you don't tightly focus on your ideal customers, these best customers will go somewhere else – to a product or service that is a better fit or a brand message that resonates more deeply. That could leave you fighting for your business's survival with mediocre, low-margin customers.

Yet, we also have a unique opportunity. By narrowing your focus on ideal customers, you will far more easily attract these customers. You can also charge higher prices and lower operating costs while delighting customers like never before.

This applies to brick-and-mortar businesses too. Even the massive, publicly traded home improvement store Home Depot could generate far greater profits by focusing attention on contractors. Their competitor Lowe's grew its business by focusing on women who loved improving their homes. Yes, they serve other customers who come into their stores, but this focus creates greater profits from their target groups.

In a sense, you can think about effective customer acquisition like a magnet. To have magnetic force, the metal needs consistent alignment of its magnetic field. With alignment, the magnetic poles both strongly attract and repel. Without it, it is just an inert lump of metal.

Businesses that try to attract everyone and avoid repelling, find themselves like that inert lump of metal. When your marketing is well aligned, it will attract a certain narrow audience, and it will also repel mostly everyone else.

If you need further validation of the value of focused marketing, here's a thought exercise: Imagine that one of your heart valves wasn't working properly. You need surgery to fix it. The first surgeon you go to describes their extensive experience – including hearts, gallbladders, appendixes; they've done it all! The second describes their experience working on hearts – including their elite heart surgery fellowships and recognition in the field. The third talks about how they specialize just on repairing that one heart valve – for a decade they have repaired three to four of those valves each week. Your specific valve problem is one in which they are intimately familiar and have done 500 cases very similar to yours. Who would you trust with your heart and your life?

Who is your ideal customer?

Once you embrace the idea of aligning your business strategy to your ideal client, you face a challenge. Who is that customer? Many businesses don't recognize who their ideal customer is.

Mine included, at one time.

In 2011, I launched an online job interview training program, targeting individual job seekers. Originally, I thought my clients would be like me, a millennial trying to advance their career. Pretty quickly, I discovered a different pattern. Most of my clients were baby boomers in management positions who never expected to lose a job or need to interview again. Following the Great Recession, they wanted help getting jobs. They signed up for my course, asked questions, got hired, and moved on from my business. I targeted my marketing to this group, and for a long time, this generated a fair volume of business. But in today's market, this was pretty generic targeting.

A colleague of mine who originally focused on writing resumes took a different, narrower approach. She focused on Executive-level professionals, increasing her pricing drastically and narrowing her message, which generated more substantial profits from a much smaller group of clients. Some years later, another company launched focused on landing jobs just at Amazon, Google, and Facebook. It was able to generate even greater profits per client (charging 5X more) than my colleague and grow many times larger.

With time, I discovered a better ideal customer from my client list. It was not an individual. Rather, it was an organization that for years used this same program to support its job-seeking clients. They valued the unique aspects of my training and paid for many students year after year. They were so comfortable to work with that they escaped my notice.

I mistakenly focused on how to make my noisiest, most difficult customers happier – often folks in unique job titles with different challenging work histories. This meant building more features to address each of their unique concerns and training customer support staff on a wide swath of topics. Instead of addressing hundreds of different questions, I should have focused on addressing exceptionally well the few critical issues for my ideal clients.

A branding agency I worked with faced a different issue. As creatives, they liked the idea of serving many different types of businesses. It seemed more fun. With this wide net approach, they were struggling to get steady business. When we looked closely at their client list, they had one group who was steadily increasing their retainers and sticking around. These were businesses applying innovative technology to professional services.

The agency positioned these client firms as premium thought leaders, and as a result, these firms were now both growing rapidly and charging more. Not surprisingly, once the branding agency focused on providing this value to this type of business, they quickly had more work than they could handle.

Unlike the case of this branding agency, often our best clients aren't the sexy ones. For example, a corporate training firm I supported was focused on helping Fortune 500-type companies develop the talents of its young people. Yet, when they looked at which firms were getting the most value and consistently (re)enrolling staff, they were regional firms of 50-100 people in "boring industries". Once they got past their ego, they realized they could serve this group of small businesses exceptionally well.

Uncovering your ideal customer:

Who are your ideal clients?

They are not the noisiest ones or the ones clamoring for your attention and handholding. Your ideal clients understand and appreciate what you do. They don't need constant attention to stick around. You can count on their business year after year.

Indicators that you may have found your ideal clients include: they represent an oversized share of revenue, stick around for a long time, understand what you do, and are happy with your offering. They feel you serve their needs exceptionally well. They may have referred you to other clients or offered a testimonial.

To find your ideal clients, start by looking at your numbers:

Which clients are the most profitable for you – they likely spend more than average and stick around for a long time. One framework for looking at your numbers is RFM – recency, frequency, and money. Sort through your database to find who bought from you recently, spends more frequently (more transactions), and spends more money than average (more dollars per transaction).

Equally important, they align with the core of what you do best. That means supporting them doesn't require a lot of one-off work and customizations, costing disproportionately more time and money.

For example, if you make the best chocolate chip cookies around, the person who wants to hire you for a wedding cake is not your ideal customer, no matter the expected payday (there are usually hidden costs for these one-offs too). Your ideal customer consistently orders your cookies every week and shares them with their friends, family, and business clients.

Reviewing your business financials, do you have accounts like this avid cookie fan?

Next, talk to your team, especially the people who work closely with your clients. Ask them who they enjoy working with most and who closes deals more easily. Of your biggest accounts, ask them who is annoying or frustrating – and eliminate them from consideration.

Look at your written testimonials and best client reviews. Who are they? What are the traits of the clients who say these things about you?

Note: If you still have trouble figuring out who your ideal client is, I would suggest getting some outside help. There is an idea called the fish-in-water effect. A fish would struggle to describe the water it swims in every day, because water is a constant part of its existence. Outsiders have perspective.

What makes you good at serving your ideal client?

Simply sharing publicly that you focus on a certain type of client will benefit your business. By declaring your allegiance, you are incurring a cost – showing less interest in everyone else. Your ideal clients will appreciate this. This is the first step to build your reputation.

The bigger opportunity is to understand why you serve this ideal customer well so that from a marketing perspective you can tell potential clients about the massive value you bring and, from an operations perspective, you invest in what best serves these ideal customers. (And, you can stop doing other, lower-returning activities that don't bring much value to this group.)

What do your ideal customers find most valuable?

You don't need to guess. Instead, ask them.

You can set up interview-type conversations. These customers love what you do and want to see you succeed. It makes sense for them to want to help. Still, if you wish to be subtle about your intentions, you could frame these conversations as check-ins. Ask the clients about working with you, why they chose you, what causes them to stick around, and how you can help them more. Create a clear enough picture to recruit other similar clients.

You can use data you already have. Do you have a collection of written testimonials or online reviews? You can manually read through the data and look for patterns. What are the qualities of your product or business that you see repeatedly mentioned? You can also upload the data into an AI platform, and ask it to summarize the dataset and highlight the main themes. If you have video testimonials or recorded video calls, you can also use AI to transcribe these conversations and add these transcripts to your data set.

You can also talk with your account reps, sales team, and people who know your customers best to get their perspectives as well.

If you are in a professional services business, you can ask potential clients to complete an intake form. This form asks questions to help you understand them better and determine their fit before you start work – invaluable for sales conversations covered elsewhere in this book. If you already use these forms, review those from your best current clients.

Be sure to filter data around ideal clients, and put aside everyone else.

If you have a large number of clients that you don't know well, you can also send out a survey to gather information. Keep it short just 2-3 questions. You might start with the Net Promoter Score question, "On a scale of 1-10, how likely are you to recommend us." Follow up with only a couple of open-ended questions. These could be, "What do you find most valuable about what we do?" or "What would you share with someone else who was considering buying from us?" as well as "How could we serve you better?" It can also be helpful to ask, "How would you describe yourself?" or "How would you describe your business?" You can again use AI to summarize the results, but you still want to read all the answers that come back – your customers' words can both inspire you and give you great phrases and angles for your marketing.

Whatever approaches you take, you are hoping to uncover who these customers are as people, why they find your offering so valuable for them – what are the results and outcomes it helps them to generate, and what mechanisms inside your offering lead to that value.

Creating the customer story

With this research, you can create a composite story for your clients. When you are done with this step, you will have a document that you can reference as you develop your marketing, hone your sales approach, and strengthen your offerings.

Take the time to write out:

1. What your ideal customer looks like

Who are your clients? (Include as much detail as you can.)

What are their characteristics? What does their world look like?

What do they see and hear, think and feel, say and do?

What matters to them?

Remember, we want to understand our clients as people so that we can speak their language. For example, if you were offering financial planning for families with young children, then you might share an analogy with Bluey or Daniel Tiger, but if your best clients are thrill-seeking entrepreneurs, you might quote Richard Branson.

When you are done with this exercise, you should be able to tell a story that talks about what your client looks like, the challenges they face, and what they care about, "Meet Joe…" Talk about their goals, values, and emotions.

Here's a short example for an online MBA admissions training course, but I encourage you to expand further:

Sunny is a 25-year-old IT manager living in a major city in India. He has always excelled academically and graduated from a top 3 university in India before landing at a prestigious firm, where he has already been promoted. He works hard and is doing well. He is the pride of his upper middle-class family. Still, he aspires to achieve more. He wants to achieve wealth by leaving India and working at a prestigious global company, either in Europe or North America. To achieve this dream, he is aiming for admission to a top 20 Global MBA program. He knows it's competitive to get admitted into one of these programs. So he is looking to hire help from someone with a prestigious reputation. Despite being relatively well paid, the $5,000 to $8,000 USD price for private coaching is beyond his reach.

2. The value you bring them

What is the problem you solve for them (their pain) and why does this problem matter?

Why would they come to you to solve it, as opposed to someone else?

How do you solve this problem?

What do they appreciate about what you provide?

Origin Story

When you are done with this exercise, you should be able to write a paragraph or essay – that focuses on, "Why we are so good at solving your problem," along with a strong thesis statement on "Here's the big why" and 3-5 main sources of value. If you want to go deeper, you can add examples and quotes from clients benefiting.

3. Why you are the right solution for them now and in the future.

What is the story behind your business? Why did you create it, and how does this story relate to your ideal customers? (Sometimes the story is your own journey, sometimes it's the story of someone else – a person or business that transformed your approach or thinking.)

How has your business evolved to match the needs of this client group?

Why are you committed to the success of this group, and how have you demonstrated that commitment?

When you are done with this exercise, you should be able to create a business origin story that will have your clients nodding their heads in approval.

An origin story has certain elements of the hero's journey: You stepped out of ordinary life to solve a problem; you faced trials. By overcoming each trial, you became stronger until you faced a major test. You made it through that test with the battle scars to prove it, and you've grown into something greater. With that growth, you are uniquely able to provide help to your clients.

Here's a short origin story example:

Born on the planet Krypton, Superman was sent to Earth by his father to escape the tragic destruction of his planet. Powered by the Earth's yellow sun, he could do things no human could. He was faster than a bullet and more powerful than a locomotive. With the guidance of his adoptive parents, Superman swore to use his powers for good to protect the people of Earth. Whether it was an earthquake or a supervillain, he could be trusted to come to the rescue.

Building resources that support your ideal clients

With this work, you can connect with your ideal clients far better. You understand their needs, wants, and desires, and how you fit into the mix. You understand how these pieces align.

This is the story you want to tell on your website, in your marketing documents, and in your sales meetings – the major challenge your ideal clients face, why you understand them, and how your solution is uniquely suited to them.

You can share case studies, stories, and testimonials that fit this profile. If you don't have these references right now, work with the closest examples you have. Over time, you can develop and highlight better-fitting examples.

Whether you give examples or use data and statistics to prove your value, remember that details matter. Use specific numbers and percentages. Use vivid details like a "white shag carpet smothered in a spilled bowl of guacamole" - a detail from a research study that was memorable enough to change the outcome of a mock legal case.

Over time, you can improve your core products, ancillary offerings, and premium products to fit this group.

ALAN CARNIOL
Coach and Author

https://EvolveGlobalPublishing.com/s/alan-carniol

BUILDING THE MACHINE

Peter Butler
Digital Marketer | Serial Business Systemiser

ABOUT THE AUTHOR: PETER BUTLER

Peter B Butler is a serial systemiser. Over thirty-nine years, in four industries and six businesses, Peter's passion has been to build the systems, workflows and processes so he can play in his happy place – 'productising' within the business.

Peter sees many business owners with great knowledge and experience. They can do wondrous things, yet they sell themselves short, or can't close enough deals.

Why?

They haven't 'productised' what they do.
They often haven't developed a sustainable, replicable 'system' to cost-effectively and consistently sell their 'widget'.

Peter's goal is to help businesses generate quality, qualified leads through a systemised, automated and personalised approach. To achieve this, he builds 'machines' that attract new business, filter and qualify prospects, and lead potential clients to be 'pre-disposed' to do business with you. By the time they speak with you, they're ready to hug you and do business with you, with credit card in hand.

Peter emphasises the significance of understanding your audience and tailoring your systems to meet their needs precisely. He believes in the power of automation to streamline operations, making sure businesses can focus on what they do best, while the backend works seamlessly. This approach not only saves time but also ensures a consistent, high-quality experience for every customer, every time.

With a focus on CRM systems, Peter underscores the necessity of maintaining a detailed, organised database of prospects and customers. This, he believes, is crucial for personalised communication and for nurturing leads through their journey to becoming loyal customers.

Overall, Peter's methods revolve around the core idea of simplification and efficiency, ensuring that businesses not only attract customers but also retain them through a thoughtful, systemised approach. His strategies are about making meaningful connections, leveraging technology for efficiency and ultimately creating a business environment where customers feel understood and valued.

A mantra Peter lives by is "Imperfect action beats perfect inaction every time".

Just start building out systems, start building your marketing, and start building your machine, then you'll be on the right journey.

In a recent conversation, I was asked: "How do you even get the time to work?"

With all my networking and events, it was a reasonable question. Before I could respond, someone else jumped in: "He doesn't have to do the actual work."

I was miffed. It's not like I do nothing. I still do mega hours. The difference is now I only work 'on' the business, not 'in' it.

How did I remove myself from that?

It was a gem I picked up from networking; the answer came in two words: systems and processes.

It didn't just happen; it took a journey – one that I'll now share with you. I guarantee you'll walk away from this chapter with one or two nuggets of your own.

FAST-TRACK YOUR BUSINESS GROWTH

Let's kick off with two subjects that are not my core business, but are learnings that helped me fast-track our business growth: system prioritisation and recruitment.

KNOW WHERE YOUR DAYS GO | PRIORITISE A SYSTEM

I started each day with an action list, then boom, it was the end of the day and my wife would ask, "How was your day?"

"Didn't get as much done as I wanted."

Sound familiar?

One day, I read something about tracking where your day goes, so I made a list of all the activities I did in a day, noting what they were related to (accounts, support, sales, business development and so on), and how long I'd spent on each one.

Then I saw it. A big part of my day was spent on support. Realisation kicked in: I could hire somebody to do that.

That first hire, a part-time web tech, alleviated some of the pain. However, emails were still coming directly to me.

Cue support portal.

It was now easy for me to view and monitor the roll-out, and to realise there were standard responses we used often and rewrote every time.

Cue a bank of over 140 pre-defined replies to common client support questions. That was just the start. It continued, developing into hundreds of messages for the build processes and SEO communications that can be selected and modified to suit any given situation.

Cue an efficient, on-point and congruent team.

Of course, we needed to be mindful of holding people accountable, with checks and balances to make sure everything's operating at the same standard.

Many years on, I have nothing to do with support, yet it's a solid cash cow.

That's our first powerful learning: Track your days. What can we pass on, or plan to pass on?

A side note: I asked my tech to do a 'position description' for his role; this is what he gave me: "Fix Peter's stuff-ups and go home feeling good about myself." Funny man!

GROWING THE TEAM | RECRUITING RIGHT

In business, people can either be our biggest assets, or our biggest bane. It comes down to hiring. Competency versus suitability.

We need competent staff with the necessary skill-sets. However, a serious consideration for the long term is attitude and ability to work within the team. Aka suitability.

Who has the time to scroll through dozens, let alone hundreds, of resumes, many of which are exaggerated? We need reliable filters.

I'm NOT an HR specialist by any means, but I have learned a thing or two from some of the industry bests and my own experiences. Following up on references with a quick phone call is gold, and you only have to ask one question: "If you could, would you rehire them?" Also, note that hiring remote staff brings new opportunities but its own set of issues.

One particularly useful filter is the "thirty-second audio". "Explain why you're the best person for the role." I used this filter once to hire a project manager–a role requiring very high attention to detail–and reiterated in the advert that if not done, it would automatically exclude applicants from consideration.

This simple task helped me target two things: the clarity of the applicant's spoken English, and their attention to detail.

There were fifty-four applicants. Four did the audio. Boom!

Of the four, two were difficult to understand–not ideal for a client-facing role. I was down to two for our initial conversation. First step, keep the conversation casual: "This is us seeing if we're suitable for you, and whether you're suitable for us." Knowing their family scenario is also helpful.

A key component after the initial interview is the competency test: can they do what they say they can do, and at what level?

The second key component is a psychometric test. Some people use DISC profiles. These are great, but I prefer the Harrison Assessment psychometric test as it gives a whole other level of detail, which I won't go into here.

The thing is this: if an applicant aligns with our team, based on their psychometric test result, we will hire them even if their competency is not quite at the level we'd like. In cases like these, we simply adjust the remuneration offer to suit. You can train people and increase their pay as needed.

Funny story, we were recruiting a new designer. They'd passed the competency test, all good. One of the attributes that showed up was that they tended to be defensive. In doing the debrief of the Harrison assessment with them, we got to the defensive section, open conversation, and you wouldn't believe it, they actually got defensive. Needless to say, they don't work with us. Defensive people don't 'own it' when they get something wrong.

I've never hired anybody without doing a Harrison Assessment; as far as I'm concerned, a psychometric test is vital.

And there's our second powerful learning: Get a hiring system in place, with filters, and always do a Harrison Assessment.

As we go on in business, we learn all sorts of little things. We have epiphanies. We make changes. I hope that sharing some of my epiphanies will impact you and add value to your business.

And now, on to my passion for creating lead-generating websites.

IDEAL USER EXPERIENCE | CUSTOMER JOURNEY

When someone comes to your website, it takes eight seconds for them to know if they're in the right place. You have to connect with them. They need to resonate with your messaging.

To paraphrase Flint McLaughlin from the MECLABS Institute®, when somebody comes to your website, you need them to give you "micro-yeses", nodding their head either physically or psychologically, at every section and stage.

Yes, I will pay attention.

Yes, I will engage deeper.

The micro-yes is a powerful psychological action that moves people along to the next stage: "Yes, I understand", and "Yes, I believe".

What we need to be aware of are the micro-yeses that are missing, in the wrong order, or that transition with insufficient force.

When looking at your website, ask yourself what your real objective is, and what the most effective way is to accomplish it. Be mindful of 'proclamations without explanations'. You will make powerful proclamations, but you must give them context and explanations.

What are the minimum requirements for an effective website?

Here's a simple checklist–our Digital Success Blueprint:

- Compelling headline
- Supporting sub-headline for context
- Hero Shot that resonates, brings an emotion or engagement
- Benefits
- Easy to contact (use a contrasting button color)
- Call-to-action (CTA) above the fold
- CTA replicated throughout the site, in the right locations
- Social proof
- Consistent branding

What next?

You've built your website and nailed the customer journey and user experience. You're getting 'some' traffic and 'some' enquiries, but not quite the amount you were hoping for.

Is it a 'traffic' problem or a 'conversion' problem?

Determine the traffic first. Know the actual visitor numbers and ascertain what traffic is 'possible' based on data. Next, see what users are really doing. Good marketers will make customer journey decisions from an understanding of the target market, and industry insights, but users sometimes take unexpected actions on a website.

Take this scenario as an example. We had a stellar website with an 'on-point' emotionally resonating hero image, two 'call-to-action' buttons centrally located, and a 'contact us' button on the top right in the menu section.

Using heat-mapping and a user-tracking tool, we determined a 10:1 click ratio favouring the 'contact us' button.

That was an astounding ratio!

Although click-throughs to the 'contact us' page were great, they weren't translating into good conversions. Visiting a Contact Us page also does not guarantee a form will be filled in (you need a 'success' page to track that). Moreover, the 'ideal' customer journey was actually to follow the 'next steps' behind the two call-to-action buttons.

Making sense?

The solution was to reword the text on those buttons. Something as simple as changing the CTA text from 'Book a Display Tour' to 'See Our Display Online' can improve the click-throughs.

Contrary to what most people think, a website is not just an online brochure, but a pivotal tool to help attract more traffic, generate more leads, close the sale, and even onboard new clients.

They should be online business 'machines'.

BE AWARE OF VANITY METRICS

You've done a social media post, and people have seen it. What's the one action you want them to take? In most instances, you want them to click the link that goes through to your website, right?

Once they've taken that action–the one you want–it's unlikely they're also going to like, comment on, or engage with your post. Instead, they've gone to your website and consumed your content, where you get to control the customer journey.

We've had increases of 4,200% in social reach. This is epic. It's 'off the charts' and a major boost in your website traffic.

So, don't be disappointed if you're not getting lots of likes and comments on your posts if those posts are intended to direct traffic to your website.

Do you want traffic to your website–or do you want vanity metrics?

BUILD YOUR CONTACT LIST | VALUE OF YOUR BUSINESS

Every business 'machine' should include building a contact list–the business database. Yet, so many business owners do not build this list at all. That's crazy!

Is this you?

You network, you interact online, you put in the hard yards–but are you building that list? Perhaps you use the revolution of social media, but nothing beats your own contactable list.

In his chapter in this book, Scott Bywater cites six reasons why email marketing is much more powerful. But, to do this, you need that list.

The other thing to consider is the value of your business! This value is in the systems and the infrastructure, its workflows, and processes, as well as the marketing assets around gaining that list.

Part of one of those marketing assets is the size and health of your contact list.

NURTURE SEQUENCE | 270K CRM AUTOMATION

I once did a presentation for a young woman who was launching as a business coach and needed a website.

I qualified her before the meeting, asked all the appropriate questions, and did the presentation. She was sold; however, in between qualifying her and doing the presentation, something had changed in her life. She wasn't able to proceed right then, so although she said yes, she also said, "I just can't do it right now, but please follow up with me."

Many people might leave it there, and not follow up, but I put her into my CRM nurture sequence. Each month, there was a prompt for me to touch base with her. And I did.

After ten months, although I felt like a stalker, I reached out again. This time, she was ready to proceed. "Wow, thank you so much," she said. She was so appreciative of my diligence.

But here's the irony.

In that ten months, she'd had to get a job and ended up as a project manager for a large, registered training organization. It turned out they needed help with their website. She did an introduction and the rest is history.

They became our single biggest dollar-value client for the past twelve years. We're talking over 270k worth of business.

My nurture sequences have evolved since then–more automation, more on-point messages, SMS prompts–but without that primitive nurture sequence back then, 270k worth of business could have been left on the table.

The moral of the story is to have systems and processes to follow up your leads because you never know what's happening in their life. Quite often, we make the decision they're not interested, but that is not necessarily the case. It certainly wasn't in this instance.

CRM | NON-NEGOTIABLE

Do you have a Customer Relationship Management (CRM) system?

I'm gobsmacked that so many business owners don't even have a CRM, or only score themselves four out of ten for using the one they do have.

Having a CRM is on par with having a website–it's crucial. Storing details on a spreadsheet just doesn't cut it.

Neither does email marketing software that's not a proper CRM. Perhaps you're already making do with it, thinking you're building a database. Technically, it is a database, but one without automations, systems, follow-ups, landing pages, funnels, nurture sequences, online payments, or social media integrations. That's the value a proper CRM adds, and building out the system assets as you go.

The value of a business is in those assets: your marketing, your website, CRM, and contact list. Even if that value is not yet apparent, and is not your focus, getting the right CRM should be.

While it's understandable for start-ups to concentrate on expenses, marketing investment is crucial. How serious are you about growing your business?

It can be easy to become overwhelmed with options, but you just need to remember that you're building the machine, one step at a time.

The exciting part happens once you get a CRM and import your contacts. Next, you convert your web forms to CRM forms–boom–all enquiries are now in your CRM. Connect your CRM to your social platforms–boom–all social leads go to the CRM. Set up a lead magnet with a nurture sequence–boom–you're qualifying leads through your website.

Then you build out your online calendar booking system to take meetings with automated reminders, making you look more professional and organised, because you are.

Now you can send out regular email broadcasts, which boost your client engagement and relationships, making you more top of mind and paving the way to getting more repeat work or more referrals.

Take one step or action at a time.

Before you know it, you'll have built out this machine, these system assets, and marketing assets–with an investment that is not as massive as you may have thought.

Getting the right CRM is the key. There is nothing worse than building out all these assets in a platform that then blows up. Or is hard to use. Or one where the pricing is not fixed.

Your CRM has to be simple to use (so it does get used), but sophisticated enough to grow as your business grows.

We do recommend Smarter CRM for these reasons; we may be biased, but with good reason.

SYSTEMS | JUST START

Any successful business has to be able to consistently deliver high-quality, cost-effective products, on time.

Whether your first system is a production or delivery system, a new Team Member Onboarding system, or a system related to your Sales or in your CRM–systemising equals success.

Our Web Build process currently has 528 individual steps held with ten stages.

Our Team Member Onboarding process currently has 59 steps in four stages.

Our Dynamic SEO Program has 389 steps overall, broken down into two core groups–initial 'static' one-off steps, and a range of repeatable 'dynamic' steps.

The CRM Onboarding process, it's just a beast.

People often ask me what software we use. It's not about the software, it's about documenting what you do. But maybe you're not wired that way. I'm blessed that I am. I systemise everything, even the barista coffee I make in the morning.

However, you can adapt! Decide on the one thing you don't want to do anymore–what is it?

Start in a notepad, or MS Word–whatever. Just make notes on your actions and every time you run through that process, add the micro-steps.

Initially, that task time will blow out, and the temptation to jump ahead and get it done will be great, but if you're serious about passing the baton, then persevere.

Use images to outline steps, but only where the images are unlikely to change soon. For example, Facebook changes constantly, so if it's a process based on actions on that platform, then any screenshots will need constant updating. Painful!

Make LOOM.com your friend. There is 100% clarity on the task at hand, plus it's quick to create and keep updated.

Use fewer words. I catch my team giving wordy instructions. Guess what? Wordy instructions don't get read, they get scanned and skipped. Keep it succinct.

Seek team feedback and input. With our New Team Member Onboarding, every new hire makes notes during the induction process, which then get checked, reviewed and updated with every new person. It's somewhat self-perpetuating.

SYSTEMology ® by David Jenyns is an excellent read. It's a great 'system' to help those not naturally systems-focused.

One of my takeaways from Jenyns' book was to find your 'systems champion' within your business. One of my project managers went on maternity leave for a short spell, but she helped me find a replacement, trained that person in her role, and continues to monitor her–so there's a system in itself. That project manager is now back full-time, and operates as my executive assistant. With her tenure with us and her experience with our workflows and processes, she is perfectly wired to be our systems champion. Boom, another self-perpetuating system.

A word of warning, as with all repetitive processes, people can tend to just get on with the task at hand and not necessarily follow the steps closely.

How do you overcome this?

Checkboxes. They are your safeguard. If someone 'ticks it' and it's not been done, you can hold them accountable.

Human nature decrees, however, that we will miss things. If and when we do, I've set this response question. Is it a people problem, or a process problem?

By approaching any issues this way, the issue then becomes a more objective conversation. As in the 'One Minute Manager'® framework of Kenneth Blanchard and Spenser Johnson: it's not personal, it's a behavior.

If it was a people problem, own it. And make sure others 'own it' if they got it wrong.

And if they won't … remember the Harrison Assessment? You'll know whether defensiveness is an intrinsic character attribute IF this shows up in the results. I won't hire if defensiveness is high, regardless of skills, competency and all other traits.

Systems are not something you set out once and leave. They are dynamic. They are continually evolving, especially if the industry has a lot of variables.

Of all the industries on the planet, the two hardest to systemise and automate are the Custom Home Builder industry and the Website industry.

Why those two?

They have the MOST variables of any other business. Every project is different. They might have the same stages, but there are variables within those stages with so many options–right from the 'go' to the 'whoa' of any project.

WRAPPING UP

There are essentially 'seven pillars' in business:

- Executive
- Office/Admin
- Marketing/Sales
- Finance
- Production
- QA
- Public Relations

As we grow our business, each of these pillars needs specific attention to attain a higher level.

In business groups, I physically 'show my hand' as being at a certain height, and then move clockwise to another pillar, and another, until I've completed a full circle. I then move my hand higher, representing working on that pillar again, taking it to a new level.

As it is in business, everything is always a work in progress. The end game is to do ourselves out of a job and have the team run the machine.

I need another chapter! There's more to say on our toolstack, widgets we use, managing teams, systemising, masterminding, networking, mentoring, strategic partnerships, and of course, my CORE business of WEB | SEO | CRM and Digital Marketing.

However, FOUR reports are available on our website. They are free, value-add reports, with no bait and no switch sales tactics.

How To Build a Website That Attracts High-Quality Clients!

Unlock the Secrets to CRM Success!

Discover the Secrets to Dramatically Boosting Your Online Visibility!

How Next Generation Marketing Turns Browsers into Buyers!

We'd love to hear from you if you found value in these reports, or if you'd like to book a demo of Smarter CRM.

May you start kicking some serious goals this year.

PETER BUTLER
Digital Marketer | Serial Business Systemiser

https://EvolveGlobalPublishing.com/s/peter-butler

SCALING UP WITHOUT MELTING DOWN - USING AUTOMATION THE SMART WAY

Melanie MacDonald
Investor and Business Advisor

ABOUT THE AUTHOR: MELANIE MACDONALD

Melanie MacDonald's journey to the BRW Fast 100 list showcases her belief that the secret to profits is in unlocking the unique puzzle in every business. Growing up in a rural town, she left home at 17 to start a degree as a veterinarian. It turned out becoming a vet involved cutting up lots of animals and not saving fluffy kittens, so she graduated instead with a degree in chemistry.

Melanie quickly rose to a senior management role within the world's largest pharmaceutical company. However, her love of a challenge led her in her 20s to the world of real estate, where she started in residential investment, then eventually commercial property and land development.

Identifying opportunities and adding value is her common theme. She founded an award-winning education business in her 30s, was listed in BRW's Fast 100 and Top 100 Business Women, and acquired then grew a national business by 800% and sold it to a publicly listed company. Another of her personal success stories includes buying a business from liquidators for 1/14th of the asking price and turning it back into a thriving venture.

Melanie's achievements have made her a sought-after speaker, author, and business growth advisor. These days (when not scuba diving or riding her horses) she does a small amount of growth consulting. She has been a finalist in businesswoman of the year awards in two countries, featured in national newspapers, and appeared on television in Australia and the USA. Her international presence includes speaking to audiences as large as 4,000 people and consulting in various countries.

At the heart of Melanie's work is her desire to open others' eyes to the concept that the opportunity of a lifetime comes along once a month, helping them distinguish between a genuine opportunity and a distraction. In her recent consulting projects she has grown businesses for the owners, then automated the processes to free up time and money. This allows the owners to step back and make other investments and reduce their financial risk.

The instant we plugged the phone in, it rang. I was halfway through my newly practised "hello this is Melanie welcome to..' and a very cranky man at the other end of the line started yelling at me.

"What is WRONG with you people? I placed my order 8 weeks ago and I still don't have it! And I've been trying to call and nobody has been answering. We have government contracts to fulfil! WHERE IS MY ORDER?!"

By the end of the first week, I had received 21 phone calls, four of them angry and shouting, and been faxed and emailed copies of overdue order forms (that I had no idea existed until they arrived) with orders totalling $120,450 in value.

Welcome to the adventure that happens when you think you have been a golden-haired girl in the corporate world and decide to become self-employed by buying a well-known, but decidedly smaller than it once was, engineering business from its liquidators. It can't be that hard to buy a broken business and fix it up. Right? Not when you've been promoted multiple times and sent all over the world to solve problems by the billion dollar company you worked for? Right?

Turns out, the significant difference between a large corporate and your own venture is availability of resources. Anyone can be clever with the company Amex. And by resources, I mean all of them. Human, financial, real estate, supplier and customer relationships, reputation and brand, the lot.

The first day I was in business for myself, I printed and put all the outgoing mail into my out tray on my desk and went home. When I came back in the morning, it was still there. Turns out, there is no mail fairy when you work for yourself. And no HR fairy to organise coverage if you want to take holidays either.

So, back to the shouty phone callers.

This was the early 2000s, and I had moved on from my corporate life and been delivering some supervisor training, mostly to blue collar manufacturing companies. I was getting a lot of pushback from the business owners, mostly about how 'this management theory bs doesn't work out here in the real world love' and it was starting to really irritate me. A wiser woman than I may have just developed her sales and marketing skills and got better at convincing the decision makers, but to me, the only option was to find and buy a failing manufacturing business and fix it up and prove myself right. Seems I was never one for choosing the sensible option…

I heard about a company in Melbourne which was being broken up and sold by the receivers/liquidators. The main company had been running since 1935 and made automotive parts. With the decline of the car manufacturing industry in Australia, it had shrunk from one of the major local employers to a fraction of its former self.

There was one smallish piece of the business which operated separately. It was still an engineering manufacturer but supplied trains and trucks with aftermarket parts instead of supplying the big car manufacturers.

The accountants were still trading it but were about to close down if they couldn't sell it for $800k. I had about $50k to my name, so I offered them that. They didn't take it. They didn't even want to write down my contact details. Oh well. Worth a try. At least they let me email them my offer.

Some months went by and I had moved to Brisbane. One sunny Tuesday in late October, my phone rang. It was the accounting firm. Was my $50k offer still valid? They had a falling out with the landlord and needed to move the whole business out of the factory before the end of the lease. Which was 5pm on Thursday. Two days away.

I said my offer still stood except if I needed to move the entire contents of a factory within 48 hours, I would need my $50k for the move. So if they could wait 12 months for payment, then yes, my offer still stood. They laughed at me (again) and hung up.

The next morning, they called back. I had a deal. As long as I could clear the factory by 5pm the next day.

After a self taught crash course that morning in such topics as 'how to hire forklifts and operators from 1776 km away' and 'what is a B Double and how many do I need' (answer: a big truck with a trailer and two should be enough) I told the truck drivers to start driving around Australia when they left Melbourne on Thursday afternoon and by the time they got to Brisbane, I would give them the unloading address.

By Friday I had leased a factory (sidebar: and learned something that made me quite a bit of money in later years — that adding a tenant to an empty commercial property immediately increases the valuation) and on Monday, we were unloaded and the phone was reconnected.

Hence all the shouty people.

Turned out, the phone lines had been unplugged for a few weeks so were just ringing out.

It also turned out that we had enough stock on hand to fill the approx $120k of orders.

It also turned out that nobody had invoiced for or paid for these lost orders as the fax was unplugged as well.

And it also turned out invoicing $120k to customers on the 1st of November while leaving the default payment terms in your invoice template from your accounting software of '7 days net' on the invoices does not mean you will be paid on the 8th of November. Which means it is a bad idea to start spending the money. Those three little letters 'net' mean it's not even due until the 8th of December and big industrial company accounts people are unsympathetic to ignorance. Plus, it turns out that getting them to pay bills in December in the lead up to the holidays is not really a thing. If you have a business that gets paid on invoice, you will know exactly what I mean.

However, we survived (just), and fast forward a couple of years and we were doing three times the revenue it had been doing before the receivership, plus I had learned to raise my invoices on the last day of the month and place my orders on the 1st!

And that's kind of where it all started, really. In the 20 years since, I've bought and sold a bunch of businesses and properties. I've learned a few key lessons which I thought I would share with you, and then in the last couple of years, with the acceleration of new technology, I've found and tested much easier ways to grow businesses fast compared to the hard manual slog of the early days. Here are the first couple:

Lesson One: Just Roll With It

I was helping a business with a crisis once and the director tearfully said to me, 'When will the problems stop?' I had to gently tell her that the answer was 'never'. You just get more experienced and better able to deal with them. The problems that used to stretch your resourcefulness become nothing, and you go looking for a bigger challenge.

Although a word of caution: some years ago I started training in technical diving (for caves and shipwrecks). An old man on a boat on a pleasure dive one day asked me why I was doing the training and I said I was bored and needed a challenge. He said, 'you know there are old divers and there are bold divers, but there are no old bold divers'. I heeded his message and went back to playing with octopuses. The same applies to business. As you get more skilled, it's easier to try to push the envelope just because you are used to it being challenging and it feels weird if it isn't stressful. Sometimes you don't need to. It's ok to have an easy life.

Lesson Two: Cash Solves Most Things

Revenue or turnover is great for the ego, but profit keeps your business sustainable and gives you quality of life. There are plenty of people with smaller, extremely profitable businesses who can't brag of a $50 million turnover but are comfortably taking home $1m plus from their $3m turnover. If I compare some of the people I know with the stressful bigger businesses to the ones with the small but profitable ones, I know whose life is easier and happier. I must be getting old, as I finally understand all those things people tried to tell me about what really matters in life. Spoiler: it's not all about the net worth. Profit combined with free time gives you great quality of life to do the things that really matter (like play with octopuses).

Let me share another story of a recent business project. You couldn't get more different from receiving faxed orders for engineering components and getting shouted at for missing parcels if you tried, and I think it's a great illustration of what is possible now.

In 2018, I had exited my most recent business project and was looking around for some ideas. Somehow I ended up down the rabbit hole of internet algorithms and targeted marketing. A lot has changed since then (internet years are sort of the opposite of dog years, aren't they?) and half of what I found out isn't possible now while the other half is common knowledge. At that time, however, very few people understood how easy it was to follow someone around the internet and promote your product to them.

At the time, if you were selling, for example, fishing rods, you could buy very targeted lists of people who were about to buy a fishing rod. This data was collated by using a combination of where the person had been, what they had searched for online, what else they had bought, and various other indicators. A person who was about to buy a fishing rod might have spent time at the lake and in a camping store (but only bought a kayak), searched for 'good fishing spots' or 'fun activities with kids' and spent time watching online videos about local fishing rules.

As most people know now, based on that combined data, you could buy an anonymised list of all the potential fishing rod buyers and set up a series of ads in the various social media platforms and on whatever websites they were viewing and chase them around the internet, changing what you showed them depending on what action they took. This was in the very early days and it was mainly big companies and politicians who were using these tools.

I flicked out an email to a few people with small businesses asking if anyone would like me to experiment with finding some more customers using some of these tools and had quite a few replies. One of those businesses is still a client (and good friend) today. They were a professional services firm who normally had over 200 clients but due to some changes in government policy had dropped to 32 clients and really needed to get back to 200 to remain viable. They were sitting on 78 with 3 months left in the year. We set an ambitious target of 300 for the following year and a 'crazy but would love it' goal of 500 clients.

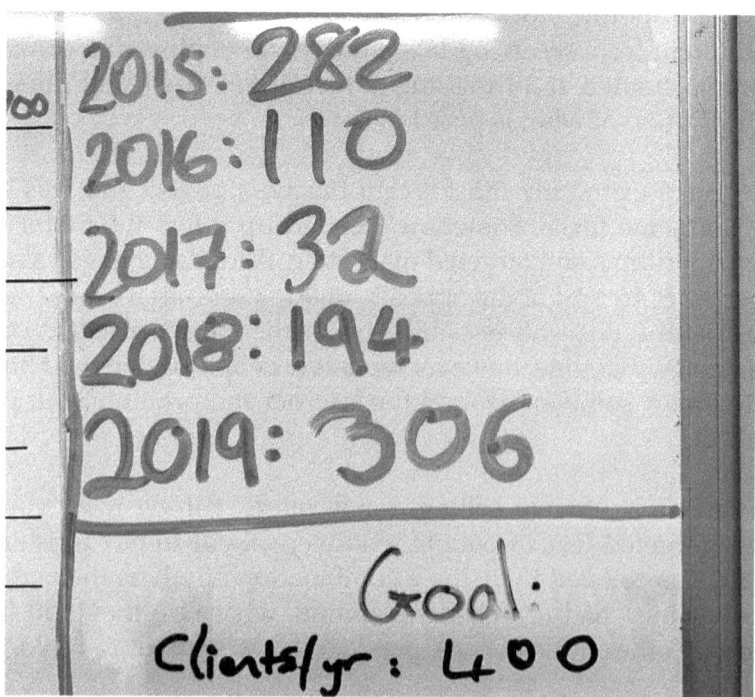

I stopped photographing their whiteboard after 2019 (some little world event happened the following year which meant we worked from home?) but they continued to grow and in the first quarter of 2023, they signed up 1600 new clients.

You are probably either thinking 'that is awesome, they made so much money,' or 'that is horrifying they must have really struggled operationally' and both of those points are completely valid!

Over that time, they grew from 7 staff to about 50, and the biggest constraint on their growth was finding the right people. The marketing process was almost completely automated so could be ramped up and down by this stage but the processing of customer work was still very manual. And there is a skills shortage in their area.

I had been staying as up to date as I could with what was happening in the world of automation and AI. We had already been using a product to create their ads which used a previous version of generative AI and then, of course, the release of ChatGPT made that whole area explode. Suddenly the problem was which tool to choose from rather than whether one existed.

The CEO has always been willing to let me experiment on their business, so the team decided to look at how many of the manual processes done by the admin team could be completely automated. This became more urgent than expected in 2023, with a combination of more rapid growth in customer numbers and some of the key admin team leaving.

They started 2023 with 7 admin staff able to onboard 20 new clients per week between them.

They finished 2023 with 2 admin staff able to onboard 20 new clients per day between them (yes per day that's not a typo).

Nobody was made redundant, no customers noticed any changes (except for the faster turnaround of their work), and the CEO was able to drop down to working 3 days per week. The admin staff get to spend their time doing the interesting parts of their jobs and all the routine boring bits just need to be checked by them. The key to it was working out how to efficiently get all the different programs and platforms to talk to each other, and where that couldn't happen just to set up routines (with simple tools such as Power Automate- the Microsoft product) where a computer could sit there and run all day logging in to websites, entering data, and sending emails.

There is still lots more to do and we are now experimenting with another section of the business to see how far we can push the AI envelope to replicate processes but improve customer service while we are at it. Smaller companies cannot afford to operate with the terrible robotic customer service that so many of the big organisations get away with so everything we do needs to improve the experience for the customer. Otherwise, we just end up with the digital version of 'Press 1 to talk to a human. There are no humans available today. Goodbye' that drives us all insane when trying to get service from certain nameless telcos and government departments.

Here are the next couple of lessons I've learned so far from this automation adventure that I thought were worth sharing:

Lesson Three: Understand Your Processes Before You Automate Them

Map your processes first and revise and improve them if necessary before you try to automate them. I spent a couple of years at the end of my corporate career working as a management systems auditor and learning how to make a flowchart of the steps that happen in any part of the business has been an incredibly helpful skill for these projects. If you don't know how to map out your processes step by step, get someone in to do it for you. IT people talk about 'garbage in, garbage out' for a reason and if you get this part right, the rest of it will be easy. Too many organisations have the organisational equivalent of the 'missing stair' and have built manual processes to get around unnecessary limitations caused by people or resource constraints. Fix those issues first before you build a faster version of the same process.

Lesson Four: Don't Get Distracted By Shiny Things

If you are like me and like 'techie things', you can very easily get overexcited by the number of tools being released every week. When ChatGPT was first released, a handful of friends and I put together a spreadsheet where we categorised and tracked as many of the new tools as we could find. One by one, my friends dropped out, citing overwhelm and told me just to let them know if I found anything amazing. Then, one by one, they asked me to stop telling them about anything at all unless it was specifically relevant to the aspect of their business they were currently working on! For about a week after that, I felt a bit sad that nobody else wanted to hear all the 'have you seen this? Did you know you can copy someone's voice and make a phone call with it?' and all the other crazy apps that were being released but within a week of the last friend dropping out, I hit the overwhelm wall myself.

It was like the early days of the internet. Somewhere I have a certificate just called 'Certificate in The Internet' from going to college and learning `The Internet'. Imagine if you had tried to keep up with every new website that was released? That's what it is like trying to stay up to date with AI and automation apps. So what is the answer?

Start with the end in mind. Start with your business and your needs and decide what you want to happen. For example, you might decide you want to have a voice-based system that will allow clients to call in 24/7 and change their appointment times. So then you can look for a tool that will do two-way communication using voice, a tool that can hold any relevant knowledge, and a tool that will integrate with your calendar. Spend the time just looking for those things rather than being distracted by every bright, shiny object.

Lesson Five: Humans Are Important

We are still in the early days of all of this. Plan to keep a 'human in the loop' for all your processes for now. For example, if your system is issuing documents to customers, have a human review all documents to start with and then review a regular sample on an ongoing basis. It's still much faster and efficient to read through a bunch of quotes and click yes or no before they are sent than it is to have to prepare each one by hand. But this way you can avoid your system doing dumb things like one of the big car dealers did recently where their AI chatbot discounted so heavily that it sold cars for $1.

Where To From Here?

If you are considering whether you could do something similar in your own business, here is where I would start:

1. Choose one task to automate completely rather than trying to automate a little bit of everything. Otherwise, the mental load of half changing every process becomes too much to handle.
2. Don't think that these tools are only for automating marketing and sales. Some of the best efficiencies we have produced have been on the operations and administration side of the business. That's probably a good place to start if you want to minimise the risk of launching something customer facing before you have thoroughly tested it.
3. Test everything! Run your existing system and your new process in parallel until you have validated that it works and you haven't missed an important step.
4. Accept that if you have a limited budget, you may not be able to automate the entire system. Focus on automating the easy 80% and keep the people doing the difficult 20%. The secondary benefit of this is you have some human eyes on the robots and they are less likely to run amok and upset customers.
5. Look at upskilling your existing staff. Who do you have with a logical brain who can work step by step through puzzles? You either need to hire someone with automation knowledge and teach them your business or take someone with your business knowledge and teach them AI/automation.

Two reasons I suggest doing it this way:

a) It's almost impossible to 'buy' someone 'off the shelf' who will come and work for a small to medium business for a reasonable salary who just happens to have the knowledge of the AI and automation tools that your business will need. Especially when you won't know which tools those are until they start work. And when the tools are changing every week.

b) If you have to teach them either your business or the tools, for most businesses there is more chance that there will be lots of online training videos on how to use the AI/automation tools than there will be lots of online training videos on exactly how your business works and what makes it unique and special and needs to be preserved. So accept that you will be allowing someone to learn as they go and reward one of your existing loyal team members with an opportunity to upskill rather than hiring some stranger who will learn on your payroll and then wander off.

One bonus lesson before I go:

Lesson Six: Continuous Learning and Adaptation

My time spent at the bottom of the sea has taught me that we humans are not as different from sharks as we think. If we don't keep moving, we will die (well, metaphorically at least).

In this time of massive rapid technological change, we don't know what jobs or businesses are going to exist in five years' time. We probably don't even know what changes will happen within the next 2-3 years. I feel like our leaders are happily going about their activities with very little thought about the impact of AI on society and the economy. For your business to thrive, you need to keep an eye on the horizon yourself.

At best, the significant increase in productivity will improve quality of life for everyone, and at worst it will concentrate the profits into fewer and fewer large companies.

My goal is to make sure the people I work with and care about come out on the up side of those changes. I wish the same for you :)

MELANIE MACDONALD
Investor and Business Advisor

https://EvolveGlobalPublishing.com/s/melanie-macdonald

CONVERTING LEADS INTO CLIENTS

Keith Banfield
Coach, Author and Professional Speaker

ABOUT THE AUTHOR: KEITH BANFIELD

Keith Banfield is a successful businessman, an international professional speaker, and one of the founding members of the Professional Speaker Association in the UK.

For over 29 years, he has been sharing his ideas, strategies, and knowledge with individuals and businesses around the world.

Keith's skill is being able to simplify what others overcomplicate, so that information is easy to understand. He has produced and co-produced many audio and video programmes. In 1994, over 38,000 copies of his first audio cassette were distributed. More recently, over 3500 students from 127 countries have purchased his online video training programmes.

Throughout the 1990s, while living in the UK, he promoted and presented his Easy Way to Sell More training courses to up to 45 salespeople per week.

In 2004, he moved to Australia and continued speaking, training, and consulting. Clients include The Good Guys, Resi Mortgage, and First National Real Estate, as well as many smaller businesses.

In 2010, he co-produced a business coaching system called Profit Mechanics.

He is currently living in Queensland, Australia and enjoys training sales teams and helping frustrated executives re-invent their careers, enjoy a better work-life balance, and become a business coach.

Imagine if you were dating someone and, on the very first date, you asked them to marry you. What are the chances they will say yes? You and I both know they are very unlikely. The reason, of course, is that they don't know, like, and trust you properly, and there's no relationship.

This is the same with selling or converting leads into clients. One of the biggest mistakes business owners and sales teams make is trying to sell too quickly, before they have built the rapport and trust.

So how do you take someone from an inquiry to trusting you enough to want to buy from you?

I think a lot of people believe that all you need is the, "gift of the gab." Oh, I've even heard people described as a "born salesperson". An interesting idea – Doctor, is it a boy or a girl? No, a salesperson!

What I'm about to share with you is that converting leads into sales or orders is a process of getting someone to know, like, and trust you. To change your focus from making a sale to helping your prospect. To achieve this, there is a sequence of specific language patterns and touch points that anyone can learn. You are not born with this knowledge.

It is not about manipulation, forcing someone to buy what they don't need or want, or just being persuasive. It is about providing a solution that fulfils a need or want that your prospect has. You want to create value and a win/win outcome so that you are providing a solution for your customer, and you are getting a new order, and starting a relationship.

Who do you want as a customer?

The starting point in any sale is to know who you want as a customer. It starts with choosing a niche, and then within that niche, there is a simple acronym that you can use, which is M.A.N. It stands for someone who has:

Money **A**uthority to buy. **N**eed or want.

So much time can be wasted trying to build a relationship with the wrong person. So, who is your ideal customer? Now, of course, once you know this, you need to really understand that person. Brainstorm with colleagues. Think about what makes that person tick. What problems are they facing? How do they feel about that? What would they really like?

Really understanding your target market is critical. It means that not only can you save money with your marketing, but when you are building the relationship and wanting to convert a new customer, it is so much easier too.

The Client Journey.

Just like with my earlier dating example, there will be a number of steps involved, from the point of someone expressing an interest in what you provide to actually buying from you.

I haven't dated for many years, but when I did, the first step in building a relationship might be a simple coffee. The next, a walk along the beach. Maybe a meal might be after that. I am sure that you have the idea…So it's like there are a number of small interactions or touch points that create a journey. Each one building rapport, trust, and a stronger relationship.

So, what does a client journey look like?

Depending on your product or service, you might need to go and visit your prospect. You may be able to do everything online using a platform such as Zoom or TEAMS. You may have a physical product that your prospect needs to see and touch. Or perhaps you could make a sale by phone.

What does the client's journey look like? Here is an example:

1. You have identified your niche – who you want as an ideal client.
2. You are marketing where they hang out.
3. You then get a lead and want to make sure they are suitable. You could do this by funneling them through a webinar or questionnaire. I prefer to offer a free 15-minute phone call, though. From that call, I can quickly see if they would be a good fit for what

I am offering. I would also inquire about who would be involved in decision making and whether they could afford to pay.
4. The next step might be a Zoom or Teams call. You may want to go and visit them instead, of course. This would normally be the time when a sale is made.

Bringing all this together involves a series of building blocks. Let's look at those.

Your mindset

How do you see yourself? I know it might seem like a strange question, but many people see themselves as not clever enough, not deserving success or not good enough. As a result, it is not uncommon for people to self-sabotage and deliberately, but unconsciously, act in a way that will stop themselves from being successful.

They will blame the weather, the traffic, the government—anyone but themselves. Of course, this behaviour pattern will repeat over and over again.

Having the right mindset is, therefore, not just important, but critical to success. Focus on your successes and what makes you good.

Are you professional?

As the saying goes, "you only have one chance to make a great first impression." So always ensure that you turn up for an appointment on time. If you are meeting someone in person, make sure you are appropriately dressed. You can check the route online in advance to see where you will park and what traffic you may encounter.

If you are conducting an online meeting, then ensure that you have a fast enough internet connection and a good-quality webcam and microphone. Ensure your surroundings are uncluttered, and you may also want to invest in an LED ring light. Lighting can make a huge difference in the clarity of the video.

I was looking at cars for sale on Marketplace and was astounded by how many people had uploaded pictures of their car interior without first cleaning debris, used drink containers, and other litter from the floor. To them, they must be so used to it being there that it is invisible. I wonder how much a simple thing like that reduces the desire of potential buyers.

Framing

Assuming that you are making a great first impression, let's look at the next step, which is framing.

If you are meeting with a prospect in person, it is useful to have an agenda. This makes you look very organised and helps to keep the meeting on track. The agenda items might include:

1. Where are you now?
2. Where would you like to be?
3. What difference will that make?
4. Roadblocks and challenges?
5. Solution?
6. Timeline?
7. Next steps?
8. Any other business.

Surprisingly, many salespeople and business owners do not have an agenda and just wing it.

Before I show you how to introduce it, there is some psychology that I need to share with you. If you want someone to do something or accept your suggestion, ask with a benefit to them. The language you could use is:

"I know we have allocated 60 minutes for this meeting. So that we can maximise our time together, I have created an agenda."

What we are doing is setting the scene for what is about to happen next.

What if you are doing an online meeting? The journey format in the agenda still applies. Essentially, we frame what we are about to say and do. Next, we ask questions to uncover the pain or problem that they are currently encountering, their needs or wants. Provide a solution in terms of the benefits they will enjoy and then explain how they can get them.

So, working online, again, we are going to frame what is about to happen. You could say…

"Am I speaking to {Prospect name}? As I understand it, the purpose of this call is to understand where you are now, where you would like to be, and to see if and how I might be able to help."

Then ask a question such as, "sound good"?

Understanding the FBP model

FBP stands for features—benefit and pain. So, let's explore that in more detail.

If you are selling something, it will have features. A simple example might be that a car has air conditioning or climate control. Your client, though, is not buying air conditioning, they are buying a cool, comfortable ride, which is the benefit. Interestingly, though, the motivator is not to stay cool; it is to avoid driving while feeling hot and sweaty, which is the pain.

Put simply, most people will want to avoid pain more than gain pleasure. For example, most people would work harder to avoid losing their job than they would to get promoted.

Now, I will come back to this later, but I wanted to mention it at this point because it will form the basis of the questions you will ask next.

Asking Questions

So, with your questions, you want to find out what your prospect needs or wants. Typically, their current pain. When you know the problem, you can supply the solution.

So, the first question is to assess the current position of your prospect. For example, you could look at where they are now.

"Tell me about your business—what do you currently do?"

Keep drilling down with your questions.

What you want to look at next is where they would like to be and why. You could also ask, "if you achieve that, what difference would that make to you? How would it help you?"

So, we have explored where they are and what they want. Now we need to look at the problems, pain, or challenges.

So, if you are doing a call or Zoom, a great question to ask would be, "what made you decide to book this call with me today?"

You could ask pain related questions such as:

- What is stopping you from getting where you said you wanted to go?
- What are the biggest challenges that you currently face with…?
- How long have you had these issues?
- What have you tried so far and how much money have you spent to overcome them?
- What's it costing you to stay as you are? (This could be a financial, time or even emotional cost.)

Let me share a sales situation I encountered, which will help illustrate my point.

I was in a large furniture chain store in the UK with some family members. We tried to get help to buy a leather lounge suite but the salespeople were just chatting to each other, so we left the store.

I could see they were potentially losing customers and money, so I contacted the head office. This led to me having a meeting with one of their directors. The questions in that meeting went along the lines of:

"If we could get all the team members properly trained so that they were maximising every opportunity, how many extra sales do you think you might make each day per store?" I can't remember the exact numbers, but let's say the answer was 10. I then asked, "roughly what does that equate to in Pounds?"

Let's say the answer was 10,000 Pounds.

My next question was, "How many stores do you have?"

Let's say the answer was 240.

My next question was, "so based on what you have told me, you are losing 10000 x 240 = 2.4Million Pounds each day by staying as you are. How do you feel about that?"

The response was, "yes, we need to do something as soon as possible. How can you help us?"

After giving my proposed solution, I was asked how quickly I could start.

To put this in perspective, at the time, in the late 1990's, I was charging 2500 pounds per day, which was almost $5000 AUD. There was absolutely no issue with that price because the pain of staying as they were was so much greater. The price is relative to the value you deliver.

Interestingly, they did not ask for brochures, proposals, or other documents. When the pain is bad enough, there is no time for that.

Imagine if you went to the dentist with an excruciating toothache. Would you ask the dentist for a proposal or brochure? I imagine you wouldn't!

Providing a solution

You may remember that earlier, I mentioned how important it is to provide a solution by talking about the benefits, results, or outcome that your prospect will enjoy.

So, you are not talking about what you do, your business, or the process. Many salespeople and business owners get confused by this.

You want to ensure you are talking about them, not yourself or your business. The language to use is, "you and your". This is so much better than speaking about "I, we or our".

So here is a blueprint for the solution.

1. Reflect on what they have just said.
2. Suggest what to do next.
3. Be assertive in your language. Use the word "let's.".
4. Provide three next steps.
5. Ask a question that will be answered with "yes".

Let me give you an example. Imagine you are a Business Coach. You might say something like, "based on what we have just discussed, what I suggest we do next is, let's explore:

- Where you are currently losing profit in your business
- Create some strategies to fix the problem and
- Build out an action plan so that you turn this around once and for all.

How does that sound?"

If that sounds like a good idea, then you can repeat part of that process.

"Great—well, let's book a date to get started then. Do you have your diary or calendar there? Which days work best for you?"

Talking Benefits

To recap, you need to talk about the outcome, solution, or benefit that your product or service will deliver. It is so easy to forget this and talk about what you provide as a list of features.

The question is, how do you talk in terms of benefits?

Here are some examples of benefits with the features at the end of the sentence. After you have read through these, I will show you how to create your own.

So that you can avoid running out boxes, I will call each month to see what your stock levels look like.

To make it easier for you to order, you have access to an online portal.

So that we can maximise our time together, I have prepared an agenda.

To save you time, the food comes pre-prepared.

So that your table is very strong and durable, it comes with steel bars under it.

So that you get better fuel consumption and save money, the car will automatically turn itself off in traffic and at red lights.

So that you have a steady flow of leads coming in, we will run a Facebook campaign for you.

To give you complete peace of mind and trouble-free motoring, all our vehicles come with a 7-year manufacturer's warranty.

Ok, so you can probably see from those examples that it is all about them, and how you can help them.

So, let's look at how you can create your own. The starting point is to use the following stems…

- "So that you can {BENEFIT}"
- "So that we can {BENEFIT}"
- "To save you time, we can…{WHAT YOU WILL DO}"
- "To save you money, we can…{WHAT YOU WILL DO}"
- "To make it easier for you, we can…{WHAT YOU WILL DO}"
- "To make it easier for you, you will get…{WHAT THEY GET}"
- You will get {FEATURE}, which means that {BENEFIT}"

Just using these will mean that you are connecting with your prospect or client so much more effectively than many of your competitors.

Why should a potential customer buy from you?

Let's face it: most businesses have competitors. You probably do, too. The questions to ask are:

1. Why should someone buy from you rather than your competitor?
2. How did they manage without you?

I was speaking to a lady recently who had a desire to set up a coffee shop. Now, you need to get the location right, because with all the costs involved, if you get it wrong, it can be a nightmare. I asked her the two questions above, and she did not know the answers.

If you want to sell your product or service and you have competitors, you need to be different. You need to create a unique selling package. So, how do you do that? Slash your prices?

The best way is to first make a list of your competitors.

Act as a customer and see what they do well and what they do badly.

Make their weaknesses your strengths.

It is not just about being the cheapest. It is about delivering great value.

A great example is Toyota. They have created reliable, well-made, and durable vehicles. They are not the cheapest, but they do give customers what they want. So, what do competitors start doing to compete? They provide vehicles loaded with lots of safety technology and back them with long, 7-year warranties to give peace of mind.

A few years ago, I was travelling from Australia to London, and to break the journey, I stopped at the Ritz Carlton in Singapore. The hotel has an interesting design feature in their swimming pool, and being a keen photographer, I went down to take a picture.

When I asked a staff member how to get there, they said that they would take me down and show me the best vantage point that their professional photographers use. I was amazed that they went to so much trouble. It really created a WOW experience.

How can you do more than is expected and create a WOW experience for your customers? How can you incorporate into that experience what your competitors do badly and make them your strengths?

How will you then incorporate those points of difference into your branding and marketing, so that customers know why they should buy from you?

Starting the Relationship

If you have framed the meeting correctly, asked the right questions to show that you really understand where your prospect currently is and what they want, you have talked about the outcome they can get and the benefits they will enjoy, then the next step is to ask for an order and start the relationship.

People used to have pages of sales closes. Essentially, all you need to do is ask, "Shall we go ahead with that then?" or "Why don't we book a date to get started then?" As soon as you have asked that question, stop talking and let them answer!

Overcoming Objections

Sometimes people create an objection to moving forward with an order because they are unclear about something, unsure if it is right for them, or if they are just going through a knee-jerk reaction.

The most common objections are:

- "I haven't got the time."
- I can't afford it."
- I need to think about it."
- I need to talk to my partner or colleague first."
- The timing is not right; can we look at this again in 3 months?"

Now, the best way to stop some of these is to build them into the presentation and, of course, pre-qualify your prospective client, as I showed you earlier.

Despite all of that planning, there will be some people who will throw up an objection.

The simple way to deal with it is to empathise with what they are thinking. You might say, "Absolutely, and it's not a problem. I can understand why you think that."

The next step is to circle back and ask, "but can I just ask you something?"

The next step is to reframe the objection.

Followed by, "If we can find a solution, can we move forward with this?"

For example, if the objection is that they can't afford it, but during the questioning, it was clear that if they stayed as they were, they would lose $50K per month. You really need to contrast one with the other and point out that they can't afford to stay as they are.

Find out with more questions what they mean by can't afford it. Is it too expensive? Do they have cash flow issues? Do they need a payment plan? Do they not believe it is worth what you are charging? Digging will help reveal the answers so that you can provide a suitable solution.

Summary

To convert leads into clients, you need to connect with your prospect, build rapport and a relationship so that you understand what they want. Talk about them, not you or your business.

Provide a solution with a clear set of outcomes. Remember, they are buying the solution, not the journey or vehicle to get there!

KEITH BANFIELD
Coach, Author and Professional Speaker

https://EvolveGlobalPublishing.com/s/keith-banfield

HOW TO UNLOCK YOUR SALES GAME!

Ari Galper
The World's Number One Authority on Trust-Based Selling

ABOUT THE AUTHOR: ARI GALPER

Ari Galper is the world's number one authority on trust-based selling and has been featured in CEO Magazine, Forbes, INC Magazine, SkyNews and the Financial Advisor Review.

As trust becomes the most important currency in the new economy, the act of selling as a dehumanizing experience, with endless "chasing" and multiple steps, has been completely reinvented and anchored in the timeless values of integrity and trust through Trust-Based Selling.

In his first best-selling book, *Unlock The Sales Game*, Ari describes his revolutionary sales approach based on getting to the truth and why shifting your mindset to deep trust, instead of "the sale" – unlocks your sales potential.

His second most popular book, *Trusted Authority*, explains how to position yourself as a "category-of-one" to your market, so you can create inbound demand, having clients pursuing you -- instead of you pursuing them.

Ari's latest book, *TRUST - In A Split Second!*, reveals the psychological and behavioural triggers you need to know to prevent potential clients from being indecisive about hiring you.

His new books launching soon include:
Doctors Don't Sell -- Neither Should You! -- this mind-blowing breakthrough book will challenge everything you know about selling.

Your prospects don't need to like you to trust you. You don't have to build a relationship to make the sale. Trust is all that matters. Doctors don't sell, and neither should you.

The *One Call Sale* (patent pending), provides a simple road map to making the sale in one single trust-based conversation... no pressure, no closing and no follow-up.

Everything you learned about selling will be turned upside down.

Ari is also the author of *Lessons From Toby*, a special book about his son Toby who has Down Syndrome, who has made a major impact on Ari's approach to teaching authenticity and trust in his Trust-Based Selling approach. More about the book here: TobysBook.com.

Join Ari on his next "Stump The Guru" livestream/podcast show and access the recordings at UnlockTheGame.com/Podcast.

You can ask him your toughest sales questions and he'll answer them live!

Get a free copy of Ari's newest book *TRUST - In A Split Second!* along with a complimentary "get new clients" consultation at AriGalper.com.

If you flick through the pages of business magazines and traditional sales training material, you will find a constant flow of messages like, 'Focus on closing the sale,' 'Overcome objections,' 'Be relentless,' 'Accept rejection as a normal part of selling,' 'Use persuasion to get useful information about your prospects' and 'Chase the sale.'

In most cases, it becomes about getting the sale at the expense of the human relationship. For the customer, this approach is transparent and all too familiar. Crossing social boundaries and adding pressure to the sales process makes it a gut-wrenching and painful process for both the seller and the buyer.

In this new economy, there is a much better way for business owners to succeed in creating new highly paid consulting clients. But it's not for everyone. You'll need to be open-minded because it may contradict everything you've been taught about selling.

It begins with moving away from the hidden agenda of focusing on making the sale. When you do this, a new world opens up for you. In other words, when you stop selling and start building authentic relationships based on trust, authenticity and integrity, the possibilities become endless. It's a whole new mindset in selling, which I call Unlock The Sales Game®.

The vast majority of traditional sales techniques contradict everything we know about what it takes to build relationships. But shouldn't selling be about creating new relationships with potential new clients? No one likes to be pushed and no one wants to talk to someone whose only agenda is to get what they want. By not focusing on the end goal of the sale, but on building trust instead with your potential clients, you can eliminate angst, negativity and frustration, and watch your consulting business grow to levels you never thought were possible.

Have you ever landed a sale without really trying to? You know what I mean; it just happened naturally without you having to force it. That unconscious process is the same as the process that I have created at the conscious level, giving you a "system" you can follow that makes the sales process effortless.

The sales "wake up" call that changed the sales game

About fifteen years ago, after spending many years studying the great sales gurus, designing sales training for major companies and completing my Master's degree in Training and Development, I had the most important sales call of my life.

At the time, I was the Sales Manager of a team of 18 at a fast-growing software company. One afternoon, I was on the phone doing an online demonstration with the top executives of an account we had been working on for nine months.

The call was going well. Extremely well. Everything was going to script – they were interested and asking me tons of questions, and I had all the answers at my fingertips. At the end of the call they thanked me profusely for my time. I still remember the Vice-President's final words: 'We'll definitely be getting back to you.'

I was so proud of how well things had gone that I could almost feel my head swell as I started to hang up the phone, but I accidentally hit the phone's mute button instead. They had not hung up, but obviously thought I had, and I could listen to the Vice-President talk to the other executives about our 'oh-so-promising' phone conversation. Here's what they said, word for word: "Okay, so we're definitely not going to go with him. But keep stringing him along, so we can get more information and strike a better deal with another company." I was devastated!

My first feeling was outrage – they had lied to me! I felt hurt and used, but the waves of rejection that swept over me were even worse. "I'm a good guy," I told myself. "I did everything right. I've studied all the best sales programs in the world. I didn't cut any corners. Why are they treating me this way?"

Then I remembered all the other times I had gotten a gut feeling that something was "off" about how a potential client was reacting to me. I could never put my finger on it, yet at some level, I knew everything

I had learned was incomplete. I'd ignored that nagging discomfort and kept on doing what I had been doing, until that wake-up call.

A lot of today's sales "gurus" would analyse that call and conclude that if a prospect lies to you, then it's okay to lie back. If they're aggressive to you, it's okay to be aggressive in return (because that's how you control the situation).

If they try to box you in, it's okay to force them into a commitment. But this buyer and seller conflict, battle or whatever else you want to call it, just felt so wrong to me. It took me a long time to figure out one basic truth that none of those "fight back" sales programs ever talked about – my sales approach at the time was all wrong!

There was something fundamentally wrong with how I was approaching selling. I needed to change. It was at this point that I was finally able to let go of the outrage and rejection and take responsibility for having tried to sell the "wrong" way. I realised that the old ways of selling had everything backwards, and this freed me to create a new sales approach with a primary focus on creating trust and removing sales pressure from the process.

Ironically, when your mindset is focused on creating trust with your potential consulting clients, sales happen naturally, without resistance.

When I think about that life-changing sales call above, I realise that the executives knew I had an agenda for that call – to encourage them to buy what I had to sell. I did it by "the book," dealt with their objections and pushed subtly to move things forward – you know the drill.

As it turned out, they were playing along. While at first I took the rejection personally, I later realised that the problem wasn't me; it was the whole dynamic of trying to make the sale.

Did it ever occur to me to think about the ways I could develop a relationship of trust with them so that we could explore what issues and problems they were trying to solve? No. Did I ever contemplate that by not knowing more about their issues and problems, I didn't know whether I could help them?

No.

Did it ever occur to me to ask them, "Where do you want to go from here?"

No.

I was on that call to make a sale, and the sales pressure I was exerting with every word made them feel it was okay to lead me on and even lie to me. Think about it: would they have lied to me if they had trusted that I wouldn't try and chase them, regardless of their decision? Probably not.

A big lesson learned: selling is all about trust. People can sense when you are more concerned about getting the consulting engagement than focusing 100 percent on their best interests. When you treat people as people, not as prospects, and reveal your trustworthiness, they will start to trust you. They will see you as a problem solver, focused solely on their needs. From there you have the basis of a long-term relationship – *the true competitive advantage in this new economy.*

Your *new* focus is to take the pressure out of the sales process to help both parties get to the truth of whether or not you're a fit together… ironically, that creates more high-quality sales!

Debunking The Old Sales Myths

I'd like to debunk a few common sales myths that are probably still wedged in the back of your mind.

Myth #1: 'Sales is a numbers game'

Of course you'll have heard that one many times and it may still be part of the way you think the sales game is played.

Guess where the "numbers game" concept came from? That notion came from a consultant making a sales call, getting rejected, and the voice in the back of their mind said: "Just make more calls."

It's supposed to be about how many calls you make and how many contacts you reach, right?

Well, I'm going to challenge you on that belief system. In this new economy, with trust being lower than ever in the marketplace, it's no longer about how many calls you make or how many contacts you reach. It's about how deep you go on each conversation.

It's about how good you are at creating trust. It's about how good you are at making a human connection in a conversation, so you can quickly and efficiently find out if it's a fit or not between you and your potential client.

This new sales mindset has superseded the "numbers game."

Myth #2: 'The sale is lost at the end of the process'

You can probably relate to spending a lot of time with a potential client in your sales process. You do everything right, then as you wait for the contract or final approval to come through, it just doesn't come in as you expected. Have you had that happen to you before?

Here's what's important: In this new economy, the sale is no longer lost at the end of the process; it's now lost at the beginning of the process.

It's actually lost at, "Hello." I'll prove it to you right now.

Let's say someone calls your office and says to you, "Hi, my name is… I'm with… we are a…" What goes through your mind in about three seconds?

Classic sales pitch, right?

It's over at "hello," isn't it?

It's time to evolve beyond the "numbers game" and focus on going deep into your conversations so you create authentic trust with your potential clients.

Usually when that experience happens, you start to blame yourself and you might say, 'I should have continued to pursue the conversation to get a next step.' You start beating yourself up and wondering why you lost the engagement towards the end of your process.

Myth #3: 'Rejection is part of the sales process'

You probably don't like rejection, but still may assume it's just an accepted part of the sales process if you want to be successful.

In other words, rejection is something we are supposed to just accept. As business owners, we're supposed to accept that we are supposed to be "thick skinned" and not let rejection affect us.

I'm going to directly challenge your thinking on that. We discovered through our many client success stories that rejection is actually triggered.

As it turns out, we discovered there are certain triggers that actually cause your potential client to put their guard up.

Imagine what your life would be like if you became aware of those triggers and removed them from your process? This could quickly lead to a major sales breakthrough in your client engagement results, literally, overnight!

I believe that Unlock The Sales Game is the only trust-based selling system in the world that can completely eliminate rejection from your sales process, while, at the same time, create an immediate increase in your new increase in new sales.

A Twist For You! Why "Follow-Up" Should Be Banned

When a potential client ends your initial conversation with: "I'll think about it", you probably feel a sense of disappointment that they didn't commit.

You tell yourself: "At least they didn't say no, there's still hope," and then you add them to your "follow-up" list.

A week of anticipation goes by, then you call them and say: "Hi, hope you're well, I'm just giving you a call to follow-up on our initial conversation…".

But what you hear next sends an ice cold shiver down your spine: "We haven't made a decision, but will let you know when we do."

That's the last thing you want to hear.

It's tempting to keep clinging to hope, but deep down, you probably knew it was over before you called them.

What's going on here?

Why can't they just tell you the truth up front? Why string you along, giving you hope they might work with you?

Why is this such a familiar pattern?

To fully explain this scenario, I would need to share a lot with you about mindset shifting, re-engineering your sales process, trust-building, and so on.

But for this brief chapter, I'll give you one powerful and easy solution so that on your next "follow-up" call, you get to the truth, rather than the typical "shut down" response.

First, never use the phrase "follow-up" in your conversations or your emails ever again.

It's a stereotypical "sales" phrase that only sales people use.

When you say: "Hi, I'm just 'following-up'…", it sends the message that you care about making the sale more than solving their problem.

Say this instead: "Hi, I'm just giving you a call to see if you have any 'feedback' on our initial conversation, as I'd like to hear about what's still on your mind about your concerns and if they are still a priority for you to solve once and for all."

That makes it all about THEM, and not about your goal of acquiring them as a new paying client.

Also, the word "feedback" elicits the truth of what they are thinking, and it avoids triggering the "wall of silence" from them.

When they feel comfortable sharing what's really on their mind, you can address their concerns and create trust.

Once you've done this, then say: "Would you be open to scheduling another conversation, so we can get more clarity of how to get control of your retirement planning?"

"Hopeium": Why You're Losing The Sale

A new potential client is referred to you or comes inbound from another source.

Something triggers inside you when that meeting approaches, I call it "hopeium".

It's a "drug" that runs through your mind and body that automatically triggers assumptions about the intentions of your prospect.

Here are some of those assumptions:

- **They'll be making a decision to solve their problem** ("Why else would they be meeting with me?")
- **They want to be educated around potential solutions to their problems** ("This allows me to show/prove my value!")
- **They're on a "shopping trip" to select an advisor** ("I better over-deliver so that I add more value than the next advisor they meet with.")

Those assumptions create actions in your mind that prepare you for what you believe their intentions are.

But what if those intentions are wrong?

What if those projected intentions are what they want you to believe, so you adapt to what they think they want?

What if they, themselves, don't really understand what they actually need?

When a prospect comes inbound, it's easy to assume they know what they want, understand what they need, and recognize you as the one for them.

We feel wanted, relevant and appreciated…. hopeium fills our veins… so we start delivering value, some free consulting and education to show them their shopping trip should end with you.

Here's the antidote to hopeium:

Your prospect thinks they know what they want, but you know, through your years of experience, it often is not the full picture and they often don't know what they actually need!

Your job is not to allow your prospect to determine the path they believe they need to solve their issues.

Doctors don't allow their patients to dictate what they think they need.

You need to be trusted at such a deep level, on the first meeting, that they relinquish control, by acknowledging you're the expert, not them.

As an expert, you're not there to sell anything.

You're there to diagnose their problems and assess whether you can help them.

When you're the advisor who can do this with insight and empathy, you never have to hear: "I want to think about it."

Instead, they should say: *"You're the one, how do we get started?"*

Get a free copy of Ari's newest book "Trust In A Split Second!" along with a complimentary "get new clients" consultation at AriGalper.com.

ARI GALPER
The World's Number One Authority on Trust-Based Selling

https://EvolveGlobalPublishing.com/s/ari-galper

CONCLUSION

There are many people who start books, but far fewer who finish them.

In a new study conducted by WordsRated, just 48% of adults finished a whole book in the last year. So congratulations, you're already in the top half of book readers, just by making it to the end of this one.

Did you enjoy the ideas in "The Big Ideas Book?"

Did they help you think differently about email marketing, strategic publishing, trust-based selling, and what automation and systems are really required to scale your business?

Now it's time to execute, and fully integrate these strategies into your business.

I encourage you to grab a pen and paper right now, draw a line down the middle, and write the name of each chapter on the left side of the line.

Then, on the right side of the line, write down the action steps you're going to take from each chapter - whether it be my tips on booking your calendar solid via email marketing, John North's ideas on building your own media company, Alan Carniol's blueprint for attracting and retaining top tier customers, Peter Butler's framework for spending more time on your business and less time in it, Melanie MacDonald's strategy for streamlining your operations, Keith Banfield's M.A.N roadmap, or Ari Galper's trust-based selling approach for building genuine relationships.

Once you've done that, I'd like to encourage you to consider doing one of two things based on Charlie Tremendous Jones's advice (who has sold more than 2,000,000 books in print in twelve languages).

He is famous for having stated that you will be the same person in five years as you are today except for the people you meet and the books you read.

If you enjoyed this book, I'd like to introduce you to some people.

If you're an experienced marketer, I'd like to invite you to apply to join the Elite Marketers tribe. This tribe is made up of seasoned marketing professionals who exchange ideas to stay on top of the latest trends and cross-refer business based on each other's individual specialties to achieve better results for their clients.

If you're a business owner who is looking to take a holistic approach to marketing, I'd like to invite you to get in touch to see how the Elite Marketers tribe can collaborate on your business to give you an edge in the marketplace.

I will leave you with this analogy.

A group of blind men stumble across an elephant for the first time.

To learn about what it is, they touch it.

The first man falls against the broad and sturdy side of the elephant, and states that the elephant is very much like a wall.

The second one, feeling the tusk, claims the elephant is like a spear.

The third takes the squirming trunk in his hands, and states with Confidence that it's like a snake.

The fourth one touches its knee and concludes the elephant is like a tree.

The fifth one touches its ear and insists the elephant is like a fan.

And the sixth grabs its swinging tail and says it's like a rope.

Which of the blind men was wrong?

None.

Based on their own subjective perception, of one part of the elephant, they were 100% correct.

But at the same time, they were mostly wrong.

I see the same thing happen with marketing all the time.

If you don't take the time to understand the whole picture, you'll give bad advice because…

You Can't See the Whole Elephant

This is where having access to a group of professionals who see business and marketing from different perspectives can give you an edge.

And that's why we created Elite Marketers.

Like to know more?

Then find out more at www.elitemarketers.com.au or scan the QR code below:

Warmly,

Scott Bywater

GLOSSARY OF TERMS

A

AI (Artificial Intelligence): Technology that simulates human intelligence processes by machines, especially computer systems, used for tasks such as learning, reasoning, problem-solving, and language processing.
Advertising: The activity or profession of producing advertisements for commercial products or services, including strategies used on platforms like social media and Google PPC (Pay-Per-Click) ads.

B

Branding: The process of creating a unique name, image, and identity for a product or business in the consumers' mind, primarily through advertising campaigns with a consistent theme.
Business Growth: The process of improving some measure of an enterprise's success, often achieved through strategies like scaling operations and implementing effective marketing tactics.

C

Client Management: The strategies and processes businesses use to manage interactions with current and potential clients, focusing on attracting dream clients and converting leads into customers.
Content Creation: The process of generating topic ideas that appeal to a target audience and creating written or visual content around those ideas, especially important in the approach of running a media company.

D

Digital Marketing: The component of marketing that utilizes the internet and online-based digital technologies to promote products and services.

Direct Response Copywriting: A type of writing that elicits an immediate response from the reader, compelling them to take a specific action such as making a purchase or signing up for a newsletter.

E

Email Marketing: The use of email to promote products or services while developing relationships with potential customers or clients. It is noted for its high ROI (Return on Investment).
Entrepreneurship: The activity of setting up a business or businesses, taking on financial risks in the hope of profit, and often involving innovative solutions and strategic planning.

F

Facebook: A social media platform used for marketing and advertising to reach a large audience, drive traffic, and engage with customers.
Financial Planning: The task of determining how a business will afford to achieve its strategic goals and objectives, often involving budgeting, forecasting, and analysis.

G

Google: A multinational technology company that specializes in Internet-related services and products, including online advertising technologies and search engine services.

I

Innovation: The process of translating an idea or invention into a good or service that creates value or for which customers will pay, often leading to significant changes in business practices.

L

Lead Generation: The initiation of consumer interest or inquiry into products or services of a business, an essential part of the sales process.
LinkedIn: A business and employment-oriented online service that operates via websites and mobile apps, primarily used for professional networking and career development.

M

Marketing Automation: The use of software and technology to automate repetitive marketing tasks, streamline processes, and improve the efficiency and effectiveness of marketing efforts.

Media Company: A company involved in the production and distribution of media content, including news, entertainment, and marketing materials, often emphasizing the creation of a strong brand identity.

N

Networking: The process of interacting with others to exchange information and develop professional or social contacts, crucial for business development and growth.

P

Pareto Principle: Also known as the 80/20 rule, it states that roughly 80% of effects come from 20% of causes. In business, this often means that 80% of profits come from 20% of customers.

R

ROI (Return on Investment): A performance measure used to evaluate the efficiency of an investment or compare the efficiency of a number of different investments.

Ridesharing: A service that arranges one-time shared rides on short notice, commonly associated with companies like Uber.

S

Sales Strategies: Plans and tactics implemented to promote and sell products or services, focusing on converting leads into clients and achieving sales targets.

Scaling Operations: The process of expanding a company's production or business operations to increase output, efficiency, and profitability.

Social Media: Websites and applications that enable users to create and share content or participate in social networking, used extensively for marketing and brand building.

T

Trust-Based Selling: A sales approach that focuses on building trust and long-term relationships with clients rather than just closing a sale.

U

Uber: A ride-hailing service that allows users to book rides using a mobile app, often cited as an example of innovation and disruptive business models.

INDEX

A

advertising 16, 40
A.I. 35, 38
applications 129
Artificial Intelligence 35
attracting dream clients 127
automation 12, 35

B

Big Ideas 4, 10, 9
branding 57
business 10
business branding 40
business growth 38

C

Client Management 127
consulting services 43
Content Creation 127, 35, 37
Converting Leads 97, 127, 129

D

Digital Marketing 79, 127
Direct Response Copywriting 128

E

effectiveness 129
Elite Marketers community 12
Email Marketing 128, 73

F

Facebook 12, 128
financial planning 42

G
Google 54

I
innovation 130, 128

L
lead generation 11

M
Marketing Automation 129
Marketing Strategies 4, 29, 44
Media Company 38, 40

N
networking 67

P
Pareto Principle 20

R
ROI 30, 128

S
Sales Strategies 129
scaling operations 127
social media 42
speed emails 10
strategies 127

T
Techniques 28
Tips 28
tools 29
Trust-Based Selling 8, 130, 11

U
Uber 9, 55, 129

THE BIG IDEAS DAY

It's no longer necessary to pay tens of thousands of dollars for a US mastermind (plus the travel and jet lag) to elevate your marketing game and connect with the brightest minds in the industry…

Because at this invite only event, you'll be sharing the room with many of the smartest marketers in Australia where you'll discover what's working right now, enjoy high-caliber networking, connect with incredible minds and have some fun.

This Is Not Your Average Marketing Meetup

Forget run-of-the-mill conferences where you're spoon-fed the same old oversimplified mantras like create an avatar, content is king, headlines are important, the money's in the list, you're only one funnel away, etc… At "The Big Ideas Day", we go beyond the oversimplified cliches and buzzwords - and deliver deep insights & nuances based on the best ideas that are working right now.If you've been to one of our past events, you know from experience what they've delivered. Now it's time to raise your expectations, because we're about to exceed them - here's the speaker lineup…

This is Why "The Big Ideas Day" is One of the Most Unique Events You'll Ever Attend

First, the room has a collaboration of other marketers and entrepreneurs who are on a similar journey to you, with similar interests and intensity… Second, it's a very giving culture.Third, the 'big ideas' will be coming at you thick and thin - so you're totally motivated from the minute you arrive until the minute you leave.What's more, in addition to the speakers, you'll be surrounded by a whole bunch of geniuses within the audience.

Learn More at *https://elitemarketers.com.au/s/events*

WHERE TO FROM HERE?

Join Elite Marketers: Elevate Your Marketing Game

Imagine being part of an exclusive global community where the best marketers come together to share their insights, collaborate on innovative projects, and shape the future of the industry. Welcome to Elite Marketers—a platform designed for top-tier marketing professionals who are dedicated to excellence and continuous growth.

Why You Should Join Elite Marketers

Access to Expert Insights

Elite Marketers offers you unparalleled access to thought leaders and industry pioneers who are at the forefront of marketing innovation. Learn from the best and stay ahead of industry trends with insights that can transform your strategies and results.

Unmatched Networking Opportunities

As a member, you'll connect with other elite marketers from around the world, expanding your professional network with like-minded individuals who are as passionate about marketing as you are. Share ideas, collaborate on groundbreaking projects, and build relationships that can take your career to new heights.

Exclusive Resource Library

Gain access to a wealth of exclusive resources tailored for top-tier marketers. Our library includes case studies, white papers, and specialized content that provide valuable knowledge and inspiration, helping you stay informed and ahead of the competition.

Participation in Webinars and Events

Engage in members-only webinars and events featuring industry experts and thought leaders. These events are designed to provide you with the latest insights, trends, and strategies, allowing you to learn, grow, and excel in your marketing career.

Elevate Your Marketing Skills

Joining Elite Marketers is more than just gaining access to resources—it's about transforming your approach to marketing. As a member of this visionary community, you will be continuously challenged and inspired to achieve excellence.

How to Join

Membership to Elite Marketers is typically by invitation or referral, ensuring our community remains exclusive and high-caliber. However, we welcome new applications from ambitious marketers who aspire to join our ranks.

Elite Marketers is where the best of the best converge—a global community of top-tier marketers shaping the future of marketing.

Take the next step in your marketing journey. Join us and elevate your game to the highest level.

Find out more at *https://elitemarketers.com.au/s/join*

www.ingramcontent.com/pod-product-compliance
Lightning Source LLC
Chambersburg PA
CBHW070817100426
42742CB00012B/2384